Reginald Rankin

Wagner's Nibelungen Ring

Done into English verse. Vol. 2

Reginald Rankin

Wagner's Nibelungen Ring
Done into English verse. Vol. 2

ISBN/EAN: 9783337386764

Printed in Europe, USA, Canada, Australia, Japan

Cover: Foto ©Thomas Meinert / pixelio.de

More available books at **www.hansebooks.com**

WAGNER'S
NIBELUNGEN RING

DONE INTO ENGLISH VERSE

BY

REGINALD RANKIN, B.A.

OF THE INNER TEMPLE ·
BARRISTER-AT-LAW

IN TWO VOLUMES

VOL. II

SIEGFRIED, AND THE
TWILIGHT OF THE GODS

LONGMANS, GREEN, AND CO.
39 PATERNOSTER ROW, LONDON
NEW YORK AND BOMBAY
1901

CONTENTS

PAGE

SIEGFRIED 3

THE TWILIGHT OF THE GODS . . 87

●

SIEGFRIED

SIEGFRIED

ACT I

DEEP in the thickets of a mazy wood—
That wood towards which the giant Fafner fled
To hide the Ring from Wotan; and 'twas
    said
By Siegrune that far beyond the east
His pillar'd gloom stretch'd on: and whither
    went
Sieglinde to avoid lord Wotan's rage
And bear her child in suffering and then die,—
There was the earth-gnome Mime's dwelling-
    place,
A cavern not hewn out by mortal hands,
Wherein Sieglinde, dying, left her boy
To Mime's kindness and the fate decreed.
Now Mime was a very cunning smith,
And loved to weld the metals to his will
Upon the massy anvil, and his hand
Was used to please the niceness of his eye;
Till one day, as he hammer'd out a sword,

He grew dissatisfied, and suddenly
He threw away his tools and made his moan.—
'O! this forced labour—aimless drudgery!
The finest blade that ever I did make!
One that would stand a giant's roughnesses
And ne'er a whit the worse; and yet this boy,
This hot-head boy for whom I 've fashioned it,
Will crumple it in two as though 'twere lead!'
So spake the dwarf, and threw the sword aside
And fixed his eyes in thought upon the ground.
'Yet,' murmured he, 'there is another blade
He would not find so easy to his hand:
If I could only forge the broken bits
Of Needful into Needful's self again,
I warrant he would never bully *him*!
But all my craft will never compass that.
O! if I could but make the boy that sword
I 'd change the tune I 've played for all these
    years,
And see some fun like other folk, ecod!'
He sunk his head, and wagged his long black
    hair.
'Somewhere in this dark forest Fafner lies,
And with his huge, fierce dragon-body guards
The hoard the Nibelungs made. Yet Siegfried's
    strength,

—Though 'tis a boy's—might overcome the
    beast's,
And then the ring is mine. But for the work
We must have Needful—Needful in the hands
Of Siegfried ; and I cannot forge the sword !'
Then Mime, with his face awry with rage,
Set to his hammering again, and cried :
'O ! 'tis forced labour, aimless drudgery !
The very best sword that I ever made
Is worthless for the scheme that's in my heart !
I go on hammering and tapping here
Because the boy will have it : I know him !
He'll smash the best I make to little bits
And curse me if I do not make enough !'
Now as he spoke the noise of feet was heard,
And Siegfried burst in, ruddy from the woods.
His dress was fashioned of the skins of deer,
And his bright auburn hair streamed down his
    back.
Around his neck a silver horn was slung,
And he was fragrant of the summer winds.
Before him shambled a huge shaggy bear,
Red-eyed and sullen : him the boy had caught
And muzzled with a halter, with intent
To frighten Mime out of his five wits.
Now when the dwarf perceived him he let drop

The sword he had in hand, and round the forge
He skipp'd in terror, whereat Siegfried laughed,
And gave the bear the rope, and urged him on
With many a woodland cry to chase the gnome
From out the makeshift sanctuaries he tried.
'Leu in! Leu in! have at him! have at him!
Tear him and eat him!   Rout the tinker out!'
With shouts of laughter so the sport went on,
Till Mime cried: 'O! take the brute away!
Why bring a bear to me?'   And Siegfried said:
'I brought a friend to aid in cowing thee:
Bruin, ask for the sword!'   Then Mime cried:
'Halt! keep the beast away! There lies the
      sword:
I finished it this morning.'   Siegfried said,·
'Thy skin is safe to-day, then.   Now, my friend,
Thy work is done.'   So Siegfried loosed the
      rope
That bound the bear, and, with a cunning flick,
Whipp'd the great creature out into the woods.
Then at last Mime left his forge, and gasped:
'Dead bears are well enough; I like thy sport:
But why bring live bears home?'
                              Siegfried sate down
Nigh overcome with laughter, and replied:
'I wanted better company than I

Can ever find at home. Therefore I went
Into the thickest woodland, and blew loud
And long upon my horn, if thus by chance
I might attract a friend. Out of a bush
A bear peered forth, and listened with a growl
To what I had to say. I liked his face
A good sight more than thine; and yet, perhaps,
Some day I'll find one I like better still.
Upon the spot I put the halter on,
And brought him here to ask thee, ruffian,
For news about my sword.' Then Mime said:
'I've ground the blade right sharp; I trow
    thou'lt like
The keenness of its edge.' Siegfried replied:
'There is no merit in the keenest edge
Put upon worthless stuff.' Whereat he bent
And tried the sword this way and that; then
    cried:
'Didst try to gull me with thy prattle, oaf?
Thou call'st this wretched riding-switch a sword?'
And Siegfried seized a hammer angrily,
And on the anvil laid the sword, and smote
Till nothing of the gleaming blade was left
But sparks of metal shining through the gloom.
Then Siegfried cried: 'There are the bits for
    thee!

Thou shameless bungler, would I 'd broken it
Over thy stupid pate! Thou braggart loon!
Shall I still listen to thine empty tales
Of giants' wars, and fights where gods fight gods,
Of mighty deeds and glorious chivalry,
The while thou botchest at thy tinkering,
Boasting thy skill with every vacant breath?
Yet when I test the work, a single stroke
Reveals its rottenness! If thou wert not
So miserable a wretch I'd use thy head
To break thy rubbish on, thou imbecile,
Thou nightmare of an imp! Thereby, perchance,
I might assuage my wrath.' Then Mime said:
'Now art thou raving like a lunatic:
Thy thanklessness, good sooth, is terrible!
If I can't make the very best at once
For this o'erbearing boy, straight he forgets
The good that I have done him this long time!
Wilt thou not think on what I told thee once
About the virtue Gratefulness? Bless me!
Thou shouldst be glad to hearken to the word
Of him who's done thee such a power of good!'
Now Siegfried turned his back upon the dwarf;
And Mime said: 'Thou dost not want to hear
More of that sort? Well, wilt have supper, then?
There's meat upon the spit, and soup a-boil—

I set it on for thee.'   And Mime went
And brought the meat to Siegfried, and the pot
Wherein the broth leaped hissing.   Then the boy
Turned not his head, but struck out furiously
And knocked his burdens flying from the hands
Of Mime, crying out : ' I 'll cook my roast
Without thy help : go, swill thy nasty soup
Alone, if thou art hungry !'   Mime cried :
' O ! what a foul return for all my care !   •
Is this affection's shameful recompense !
I reared thee from a tiny puling child,
Swathed thy small body in the warmest stuffs,
Brought thee good food and drink, and guarded
       thee
As mine own life.   And when thou bigger wert
I waited on thy nod, and made thy bed
As soft as a princess's.   Toys I made,
And a fine noisy horn.   Ay, naught there was
I would not do to gratify thy whims.
I taught thee all the book-learning I had,
And showed thee how to use thy mother-wit.
I sat at home all day and toil'd and moil'd
Whilst thou didst gad about the countryside.
I 've worked my fingers to the bone for thee,
And now I 'm getting old—a poor old dwarf !
For all my worry this is my reward—

Abuse and hate from thee !' So Mime ceased,
And broke into a chorus of loud sobs.
Then Siegfried look'd the dwarf straight in the
      eyes,
And answered, ' Mime, thou hast taught me much,
And much I've learned from thee ; and yet the
      thing
That thou wast ever readiest to teach
I was least apt to learn—how to endure
Thy very self.   Dost thou bring food and drink?
I feed on loathing.   Dost thou spread for me
An easy bed ?   Sleep wanders from mine eyes.
Dost thou attempt the sharpening of my wits ?
I would be deaf and dumb.   From morn till eve
Evil appears to me in all thou dost.
Dost stand ?   'Tis all alike—dost come ? dost
      move ?
Dost nod and knuckle, blinking like an owl ?
O how I'd like to seize the nodder's nape
And hurl the ugly blinker down to Hell !
That's how, my friend, I've learned to bear with
      thee.
But tell me more, since thou art really wise,
Something I've tried to puzzle out in vain—
How comes it, though I rush into the woods
Bent upon leaving thee, that I return ?

I love the very beasts far more than thee,
And trees and birds and fishes; how is it
That I come back?   Now if thou art so wise
Thou wilt declare this hidden thing to me.'
Then Mime sate him down and made reply :
' My child, how dear I am unto thy heart
This clearly teaches thee.' But Siegfried laugh'd,
Crying : ' I cannot bear thee ; don't forget
The truth so easily !'   Then Mime said :
' This is thy wilfulness, which thou shouldst
      tame.
The young long ever for the parent nest ;
That longing's name is love ; so longest thou
For me, so lovest Mime, and must love.
Just as the old bird cherishes her young
Before the fledglings find their wings to fly,
So careful Mime cherishes thy youth.
For thus the rule is written.'   Siegfried said :
' Well, Mime, since thou knowest everything,
Unfold me one thing more.   The birds did
      sing
So bravely in the springtime, that their songs
Allured them to each other; thou thyself
Told'st me in answer to my questionings
That they were wedded as are man and wife.
They kiss'd so lovingly, and parted ne'er ;

They built a nest, and hatched their young
    therein ;
And one day, when the fledglings flutter'd out,
They both did tend the brood. And in the
    brake
The mated roes lay quiet; quiet lay
The foxes and the wolves.   The father brought
Food to the lair, the mother fed the cubs.
'Twas thus I reason'd out what love must be,
And ceased to steal the young ones from their
    dam.
Tell me, then, Mime, where is thy true love,
That I may call her Mother ?'

                       Mime snarled :
' What 's that to thee ?   Thou stupid addlepate !
Dost haply think thyself a bird or fox ?'
Him Siegfried answered : 'Nay, but thou hast
    rear'd
A puling child, a little wretch hast clad :
How camest thou to get the tiny mite ?
Didst thou produce me without mother-help ?'
Then Mime, puzzled, answer'd : 'Thou must
    trust
To what I tell thee.   I am both in one—
Thy father and thy mother.'   Siegfried cried :
'Thou liest, ugly gawk !   How like the young

Are to their parents I myself have seen,
And seen it joyfully.   In the clear brook
I've watch'd the tall trees mirror'd, and the
        beasts,
And blue and clouds, just as they look to-day,
But dancing with the water.   And I saw
Mine own face; but how different from thine!
Thou mightst as well compare a glittering fish
With some fat toad; dost ever think a toad
Could have a fish for son?'
                        Then Mime said:
'Thou babblest foolishness!'   And Siegfried
        cried:
'Ha! now I've found out what so long in vain
I racked my brain to know—why I returned
When once I'd run away into the woods.
It is from thee that I must learn the truth;
Tell me my father's and my mother's names!'
From him shrank Mime, muttering the while:
'This "Father," "Mother," 'tis but idle talk!'
But Siegfried seized him by the throat, and cried:
'Then I will force thee!   Kindliness avails
Nothing with such as thee!   Yea, hardly speech
Should I have learned unless by might and main
I'd wrung the teaching from thee!   Rascal, say,
What are my father and my mother called?'

Then Mime, choking, rocked himself and wailed:
'O thou hast nearly killed me! Let me go!
The knowledge that thou covetest I'll give
Exactly as I know it. Thankless boy!
Listen and learn the reason of thy hate!
Thy sire I am not, nor of blood of thine,
And yet thou owest everything to me.
Thou art no kin to me—thine only friend,
'Twas pity only made me shield thee here—
And now my love is preciously repaid!
O fool! thrice fool! to hope for gratitude!
Once in yon woodland wild I heard a cry:
A woman lay there moaning. Her I helped
To reach this cavern here, and by the fire
She stayed beneath my guarding. In her womb
She bare a child, and him with pain and tears
She brought forth here: she writhed in agony;
I helped her all I could; stark misery
Laid hold on her. She died; but Siegfried lived.'
And Siegfried said: 'Did then my mother die
Because of me?' Mime took up the tale:
'Into my charge she gave thee; willingly
I took the child from her. Ah! how much work
Hath Mime done for thee! What sacrifice
Hath not the good man made in thy behalf!
I reared thee from a tiny puling child.' . . .

Then Siegfried broke in: 'That, methinks, is
    stale:
Tell me, who called me Siegfried?' Mime said:
'Thy mother told me I must call thee so;
As Siegfried thou didst thrive amazingly.
I swathed thy body in the warmest stuffs.' . . .
'What was my mother's name?' 'That scarce I
    know.
I brought thee food and drink.' . . . 'But thou
    shalt say!
Tell me her name!' 'Perchance it is forgot—
Yet hold! Sieglinde was the woman's name
Who in her sorrow gave thee up to me.
As mine own life I guarded thee.' . . . 'Now
    say,
What was my father called?' Then Mime
    scowled:
'His face I never saw! And Siegfried said:
'But yet my mother must have told his name?'
'That he was slain she said, and no word more.
Thee, fatherless, she gave into my charge
To keep and cherish. When thou bigger wert
I waited on thy nod, and made thy bed
As soft as a princess's.' . . . 'O be done
With that unending starling-song of thine!
Can I believe thee? Art thou not a liar?

If not, then give some proof!'   And Mime asked :
'What testimony shall suffice for thee ?'
And Siegfried said : 'Mine ears will not believe ;
Mine eyes alone can judge; what sign hast thou ?'
Then Mime thought awhile, then went and
    fetched
The two jagged pieces of a broken sword.
'Thy mother gave me these, of toil and care
The meagre recompense.   'Tis little enow—
Only a broken sword !   Thy sire, she said,
Had swung it in that last fight where he died.'
Then Siegfried cried : 'And thou shalt weld anew
These fragments for me ; mine own sword I 'll
    swing !
Bestir thee, Mime, look alive for once !
If thou art worth a rap, display thy skill,
And seek not to deceive me with some toy :
I 'll only have these pieces.   If I find
That thou art idle or dost scamp thy work,
Or if a single flaw doth mar the blade,
I 'll hammer out thy body handsomely,
And put a proper burnish on thy back !
To-day, I swear it, I will have my sword ;
Henceforward I 'll be armed.'   And Mime said :
'Why must thou have this sword of thine to-day ?'
Him Siegfried answered : 'I am going away

Out of the woods into the wide, wide world.
I never shall come back. How glad I am
That I am free at last! Naught hinders me—
My father thou art not; my home's afar;
Thy hearth is not my house; not mine thy roof.
As the fish joyously darts up the stream,
As the finch hovers at will o'er the flood,
So pass I away; like the wind in the woods
I am lost in their depths. I shall see thee no
    more.'
So Siegfried spake, and rushed into the glade.
And Mime cried out loudly: 'Siegfried! stop!
Come back! come back! I want thee!
Ah me! he's gone, and I am left alone!
A new distress is heaped upon my woes!
I am undone; how can I help myself?
How can I get him back to work my will
On Fafner? Oh! how ever shall I forge
The fragments of that most malicious steel?
No furnace ever made would melt them down!
My puny tools will never vanquish them!
Nothing avails a Nibelung's toil and sweat
'Gainst Needful; I can never weld the sword!'
So moaned the dwarf, and crouched down on his
    stool.
Now from the wood behold lord Wotan come

And walk towards the cavern.   In his hand
A spear as staff he held, and dark-blue robes
Hung low about his form.   ' Hail, crafty smith ! '
He cried to Mime : ' can a wayworn guest
Find hospitality beside thy hearth ? '
Then Mime jumped up terrified, and said :
' Who is it seeks me in the hidden wilds ?
Who 's tracked me down across the forest waste ? '
And Wotan said : ' Men call me Wanderer,
For I have wandered far.   The earth's broad
      back
I 've roamed in many a lonely pilgrimage.'
Him Mime answered : ' Roam still further, then,
And stay not here ; thy name is *Wanderer.*'
And Wotan said : ' With good men I have stayed,
Partaking of their hospitality.
He evil fears who evil is himself.'
Said Mime : ' Evil ever lives with me ;
Dost wish to add to it ? '   And Wotan said :
' The book of knowledge is unsealed to me ;
I 've left no realm of learning unexplored ;
To one I can unfold all mysteries,
And quell the torture of another's woe.'
And Mime said : ' A matchless tracker thou,
Who doubtless hast gone spying everywhere !
But here I want no trackers and no spies.

I want to be alone, and live alone;
To tramps I leave their tramping.' Wotan said :
'Many have deemed them wise, though ignorant
Of their necessities. And oftentimes
Advantage has attended on my help.'
And Mime answered : ' Ay, but there are some
Who know what's useless to them. I, for one,
Know all I want to know; my own headpiece
Is good enough for me; I want no more.
A pleasant journey to ye, Wiseacre !'
Then Wotan sate down by the fire and said :
' Here by thine hearth I sit, and stake my head
As gage in the arbitrament of words;
I place it in thy power; thine it is
If thou canst ask me aught that in reply
I cannot tell as thou wouldst have it told.'
Then Mime was perplexed, and muttered low :
' How ever shall I rid me of this rogue ?
I must be wily in my argument.'
Then out aloud he said : ' Against my hearth
Thine head is staked; be careful now, my friend,
Or thou wilt lose it ! I am going to ask
Three questions.' Wotan answered : ' Then
      three times
I will reply.' And Mime thought, then said :
' Thou 'st roamed in many a lonely pilgrimage

The earth's broad back; thou'st wandered o'er
    the world;
Tell me what people burrow in earth's depths?'
And Wotan answered him: 'The Nibelungs
Do burrow in earth's depths, called Nibelheim.
Dark elves are they, and them dark Alberich
Once ruled as lord; he tamed the· industrious
    race
By the compelling magic of a ring.
For him they raised a glistening golden hoard,
Wherewith he was to conquer all the world.
What dost thou next require?'   And Mime said:
'Much knowledge hast thou of earth's secret
    parts;
But say what race it is that sojourneth
Upon the surface of the earth's broad back?'
And Wotan answered: 'On the earth's broad
    back
Flourish the giant-race, and Riesenheim
Is what they call their country.   Twain there
    were—
Fasolt and Fafner—chiefs of that rude tribe,
Who coveted the Nibelung's influence.
From him they won the power-giving hoard,
And therewith stole the ring. But strife broke out
Between the brethren: Fasolt bit the dust;

And even now doth Fafner guard the hoard,
Disguised as a fierce dragon.   Ask again.'
Then Mime spoke, as though deep sunk in
    thought:
'Much, Wanderer, hast thou told me of the
    earth
And of the race that dwells on her rough back;
Now tell me true, what race is it that dwells
Upon the cloudy heights?'   Then Wotan said:
'The gods' abode is on the cloudy heights;
Their home is called Valhalla.   Radiant
With light and beauty are they, radiant
Is Wotan, who commands the heavenly host.
Out of the holy wood of the world-ash
He shaped himself a shaft: the tree is dead,
But the spear withers not; its point prevails
To hold the world in thrall.   Legends and runes
Are written deep thereon.   The mastery
Of the whole world he holds within his hand
Who wields the wondrous spear that Wotan
    grasps.
The Nibelungs bow before him; he has tamed
The haughty giant-brood; all things obey
The overwhelming power of the spear.'
Now, as he spake, lord Wotan struck the spear
Upon the ground, as though by accident,

And distant thunder rumbled through the air.
Thereat the dwarf grew pallid with affright.
And Wotan asked him : 'Tell me, crafty smith,
Have I divined thy questionings aright?
Is mine head still my own?'   And Mime said,
Not looking at his guest for very fear :
'Thine answers were all right, and so's thine
      head ;
And now, Sir Wanderer, fare upon thy way !'
But Wotan said : 'Methinks thou shouldst have
      asked
What boots thyself; my head was warranty
For my replies; but since thou hast ignored
Thine own concerns, we'll make thine head the
      gage.
A grudging greeting didst thou give thy guest ;
Into thy power I put my head to gain
The hospitality thou didst deny.
Now on the wager's issue thou art staked ;
My questions will be very difficult,
So brace thy mind, friend Mime, for the fray !'
Then Mime, cowed and awestruck, answered
      him :
'Long time I've shunned the land where I was
      born ;
Long since I left the womb of mother earth ;

The glance of Wotan's eye is fixed on me;
It fills the cave with light; my mother wit
Shrivels before its gaze.   Yet I must try
To rede aright.   Begin thy questionings!
By some good chance the dwarf may keep his
        head.'
Then Wotan: 'Tell me first, my honest dwarf,
What race lord Wotan treated shamefully,
Although he loved it better than the rest?'
Then Mime answered: 'Little do I hear
Of heroes and such like, and yet perchance
The answer I can give.   The Volsungs are
The love-children of Wotan, whom he loved,
Although he showed them harshness.   Twain of
        them
Were Siegmund and Sieglinde, twins in birth,
And twins in wild despair; their son, Siegfried,
Is far the strongest of the Volsung stock.
Wanderer, I prithee, do I keep my head?'
Him Wotan answered: 'Thou hast well described
The annals of that race: thou art acquit
Of the first task; a second waits thee now.
Siegfried is guarded by a Nibelung
For whom he is to compass Fafner's death,
That the smug dwarf may carry off the ring
And be the master of the gleaming hoard.

Dost know what sword Siegfried must take with
    him
If he would kill the dragon?'   Mime said:
'Needful the sword hight; into an ash stem
'Twas thrust by Wotan; only he could own
The sword who dragged it forth.   Heroes galore
Tried fruitlessly; Siegmund alone prevailed,
And carried it in battle till the spear
Of Wotan shivered it.   A cunning smith
Doth keep the pieces, for full well he knows
That only with lord Wotan's wondrous sword
Can that bold, stupid boy, by name Siegfried,
O'ercome the dragon.   Is my head still safe?'
Wotan replied: 'In truth, of all the wise
Thou must be far the wisest; where's thy peer
In cleverness?   And since this cleverness
Hath used the hero-boy in thy designs,
This third inquiry I will put to thee!
Tell me, thou crafty armourer, who will weld
The stubborn fragments of the broken sword?'
Then Mime started up in great affright:
'The fragments of the sword?   Alas! alas!
O how shall I begin?   What can I say?
Accursèd sword! why did I covet thee?
It has entangled me in pain and woe;
The steel is proof against my hammerings;

Solder and rivets are no good at all !
The cunning'st of smiths is at a loss ;
If I can't forge the sword, bless me, who can ?
That is a question I should like to know ! '
Then Wotan rose up from the hearth, and said :
' Thrice didst thou ask, and thrice I answered
    thee ;
To idle fancies thine inquiries turned ;
Thou didst not reck of what might profit thee.
Now thou art mad because it is divined.
Thy knowing head is forfeit. Thou art doomed.
Bold vanquisher of Fafner, hear my words.
He who the pangs of fear hath never known
Alone can forge my Needful sword anew.
Thy cunning head guard well ; 'tis forfeited
To him who knows not what it is to fear.'
So, laughing, Wotan vanished in the wood.

Low on the stool behind the anvil sunk,
Mime sate staring down the sunny glade.
Long time he held his peace, while shiverings,
As though of mortal terror, racked his frame.
At length he spake : ' O thou accursèd light !
Hast set the air afire ? What quiverings
And flickerings do I see ? What whirls and
    swirls

And weaves and eddies round me? There it is,
A-glimmering and a-glistening in the sun!
What hummings, buzzings, hissings fill mine
 ears!
Hither it groans and blusters; with a crash
'Tis bursting through the wood; where can I
 flee?
A horrid throat looms for me; dragons' teeth
Will tear me! Fafner! Fafner!' With a shriek
The dwarf fell prone behind the massy forge.
Then from the brake broke Siegfried, crying out,
'Ho there! thou fumbler! hast thou finished it?
Quick! where's my sword?' He went in and
 stood still.
'Where is the smith gone? Hath he run away?
Ho! Mime, mummer, where's thy hiding-place!'
Then from behind the anvil Mime spake
With feeble voice: 'Boy, dost thou come alone?'
Siegfried replied: 'Behind the anvil? Say!
What dost thou there? Is my sword good and
 sharp?'
And Mime said: 'The sword? the sword? Ah!
 me,
I cannot weld it: "Only he who fear
Hath never felt can Needful forge anew."'
Then Siegfried cried out angrily: 'Wilt say?

Or must I make thee? Mime answered him:
'What can I tell thee? I have staked mine
    head,
And lost, to him who hath not learned to fear.'
'What lies are these? Art trying to escape?'
Cried Siegfried. And the Nibelung muttered
    low:
'From him I'd flee who understandeth fear;
But that's a lesson I forgot to teach.
The chiefest of all lessons I forgot:
He should have learned to love me. My mis-
    take,
Is coming home to roost. How teach him fear?'
Then Siegfried roughly seized the dwarf and
    cried:
'Ha! must I help thee? Art thou daft to-day?'
And Mime answered him: 'It was for thee
That I was sunk in thought; how best to teach
A thing to profit thee.' Then Siegfried laughed:
'Almost beneath the settle wast thou sunk!
What profit didst thou find there?' Mime said:
'I learned to fear, that I might teach it thee.'
'What is this "fear"?' asked Siegfried. Mime
    said:
'Thou dost not know it yet, and yet wouldst go
Out of the woods into the wide, wide world?

The best sword ever made would naught avail
If thou of fear wast ignorant!'   Siegfried
Cried angrily: 'What stuff art talking now?'
'It is thy mother's counsel,' said the dwarf.
'What's good and right I must impart to thee;
Into a treacherous world thou must not go
Before thou'st learned what fear is.'   Siegfried
      said:
'Is it an art?   Why don't I know it, then?
Come! out with it!   Tell me what "fearing" is.'
And Mime said: 'Hast never felt, at eve
In the dark forest depths, when twilight falls
Upon some gloomy spot, and from afar
The wind sounds like a shriek, and dreadful
      roars
Of thunder burst above thee, and the air
Dances with flickering flashes, and the trees
Grope for thy body with their swaying boughs,
Then hast not felt Death's gruesome terrors seize
Upon thy limbs?—weird vehement shudderings
Assail thy body; senses swim and fail;
Within thy breast the faint pulsating heart
Throbs nervously; if this thou'st never felt,
To fear indeed thou art a stranger yet.'
And Siegfried answered: 'Strange, ay, passing
      strange,

This story is thou tellest.   Firm and strong
I feel my heart within me; all this dread
And shuddering and heat and giddiness
And hammering and throbbing—much I 'd give
To feel what it is like.   What canst thou do
To help me to the knowledge?'   Mime said:
' Leave it to me; I 'll find a way for thee;
I 've thought the matter out.   A dragon-beast
Hath hundreds winded, tracked, pulled down,
        and slain;
Fafner will teach thee fear, if thou wilt come
To where he ravens.'   Siegfried answered him:
' Where is his lair?'   ' Hate-cavern is it called,'
Said Mime; 'and it lies towards the dawn,
Beyond the wood's dark fringe.'   Then Siegfried
        said:
' It cannot be far distant from the world?'
' Yes, they are close together,' said the dwarf.
' Thither then guide me,' said Siegfried; ' I 'll
        learn
What fear is, and thereafter see the world!
So quickly shape my weapon, in the world
I will assay it.'   Mime groaned: 'The sword?
Alack! alack!'   Then Siegfried shouted loud:
' Get to thy smithy!   Mind what thou 'rt about!'
And Mime whined: ' O thou thrice-cursèd steel!

I cannot even botch thee! Dwarfish skill
Is powerless 'gainst thy magic. He who fear
Knows not might sooner find a way with thee.'
And Siegfried said: 'Fine lies the sluggard
    tells;
He should confess his bungling, but instead
He slyly lies himself out of his fault.
Give me the pieces! Bungler, out with thee!
My father's blade will let me fashion it;
Myself I'll weld the sword!' He spake, and
    stripped
His body to the waist. Then Mime said:
'Hadst thou the art industriously plied
Thou mightst accomplish somewhat, but to
    learn
Backward thou ever wast: how canst thou hope
To do it rightly?' Siegfried answered him:
'The task the master cannot carry out
The 'prentice will accomplish. Go away,
And meddle not with me, or else, perchance,
Thy carcass may prove fuel for my fire!'
So saying, Siegfried heaped the furnace high
With coal, and blew the bellows lustily,
Then fixed the broken sword-blade in a vice
And filed the bits to powder. Mime cried:
'What art thou doing? Use the solder, boy!

'Tis fused for thee already ! ' Siegfried said :
' I do not want thy solder ! Such like trash
Is useless in my forging.' Mime whined :
' Thou hast destroyed the file, and spoiled the
 rasp ;
Wilt thou the sword itself annihilate ? '
Siegfried replied : ' The sword shall turn to
 dust ;
Thus shall I conquer it.' And Mime said,
While Siegfried filed away with might and
 main :
' Here cleverness is nothing ; that I see :
Stupidity befriends the ignorant !
How he doth work ! The steel gives in to him,
Although no hair he turns. Were I as old
As this my cavern and the encircling woods,
I never should have seen so strange a sight.
The sword he 'll conquer ; that is evident :
Fearless he 'll weld it to perfection point ;
The Wanderer knew all. How shall I hide
My 'minished head ? It is the bold boy's prize
Unless by Fafner he be taught to fear.
Alas ! poor me ! For if he doth learn fear
How can he slay the dragon ? How shall I
Obtain the ring ? Accursèd double-plot !
It doth enthrall me, if I find no means

To make a tool of fearlessness itself!'
Then Siegfried, having filed the sword to dust,
Put the rare powder in a crucible,
And said : ' Ho, Mime! quickly tell me true
How hight the sword that I have wrought to
    dust ? '
And Mime said : ' Needful thy sword was
    named ;
So said thy lady-mother.'   Siegfried cried:
' O Needful! Needful! notablest of swords !
Why did I have to file thee into dust ?
Thy bright, keen beauty I have worn to shreds ;
The crucible must hold thee !   Bellows, blow !
Fan the white heat !   Wild in the forest grew
The tree I felled, and from the dark wood burned
The charcoal heaped in piles beside the hearth,
Blow, bellows, blow ! and fan the hot white
    glow !
How gloriously the old tree turns to coal !
How bright and clear it burneth !   Leaping sparks
Dart from it, and eat up what was a sword.
Hoho! Hoho! blow, bellows, blow !   Hoho!
Fan the hot glow !   O Needful, notablest
Of swords ! thy dust is smelted ; in thy sweat
Thou swimmest now ; soon shalt thou swing
    again

As mine own sword!' Then Mime muttered
   low:
'The sword he'll forge, and Fafner will he slay;
That I can see for certain. Hoard and ring
He'll win him in the conflict; how shall I
Obtain the prizes? Wit and cunning both
May plunder from him, and my head preserve.
Weary with fighting he will crave a drink;
That drink from deadly juices I will brew.
He need but drink one drop; swift into sleep
He'll sink, and with the weapon he hath won
I'll cut him from my path, and seize the spoil.
Ha! thou wise Wanderer! didst thou think me
   dull?
How dost thou like this keen-edged scheme o'
   mine?
Methinks I've found a way out.' Thus he spake,
And springing up in glee he brought some jugs,
And out of them poured juices in a pot.
Meanwhile Siegfried the molten steel had poured
Into a mould, and plunged it in the tank,
So that the metal hissed. And Siegfried said:
'A fiery stream assailed the water's depths,
And frenzied rage hissed up; the biting cold
Tamed the fierce steel. As though to sear it flowed
Into the water; now it flows no more.

Rigid it lies, and stiff, my lordly sword,
Haply hot blood will flow about thee soon !
Now sweat once more, that I may fashion thee,
Needful, of swords most notable !'   He spake,
And thrust the sword among the glowing coals.
Then to the dwarf he turned, who on the fire
Had set his little pipkin, and cried out :
' What doth the clown with pots ? While I burn
     steel
Art thou soup-brewing ?'   Mime answered him :
' The smith is brought to shame ; the 'prentice
     hand
Informs the master's : since a life-time's craft
Hath passed away from me, I 'll be thy cook ;
While thou art making broth of iron I 'll whip
Some eggs into a soup.'   And Siegfried said,
The whiles he laboured at his hammering :
' Mime the craftsman plays at cookery !
Smith's work he doth not fancy ; I have smashed
All his fine swords !   I am not going to touch
The stuff he 's cooking. He would have me learn
The way to fear : I 'll learn that craft elsewhere ;
Do what he will he shall not teach it me,
For he 's a wretched bungler. Ho ! Oho !
Forge me a tough blade, hammer ! Ho ! Oho !
Oho ! Hahei !   Upon a time thy blue

Was dyed with blood; its red gouts made thee
    red :
Chill was thy laughter, cold didst thou lick up
What was so warm ! Oho ! Hahei ! Oho !
To-day thy red is from the glowing fire ;
Thy yielding toughness to my hammer bows ;
Thou spittest sparks at me ; thou art enraged
That I have tamed thy mettle ! Ho ! Oho !
Forge me a tough blade, hammer ! Ho ! Oho !
I love these merry sparks ! A touch of rage
Adorns the bold ; thy face is laughing now,
But very grim and grisly canst thou look !
Oho ! Hahei ! Oho ! The task is done
By dint of fire and hammer ! With strong blows
I conquered thee ; now let thy red blush fade,
And cold and hard be thou. Oho ! Hahei !'
So sang Siegfried, and plunged the glowing steel
Into the tank, and laughed to hear it hiss.
Now, while the boy was busied in the task
Of fitting hilt to sword-blade, Mime said :
' He hath contrived a sword with which to slay
Fafner, my enemy ; and I have brewed
A potion that shall conquer Fafner's lord.
Success is bound to crown my stratagem !
Safe is the smiling guerdon of my toils !
The thing my brother made, the shimmering hoop,

Through which resistless might he exercised;
The light, clear gold, that makes a man a god—
'Tis mine; I 've won it; all its strength is mine!
Alb'rich himself, who held me in his bonds,
I will reduce to socage; Nibelheim,
With all its hosts, shall own me as its lord.
How they will honour the despised old dwarf!
Heroes and gods will throng towards the hoard;
Before my nod the world itself will bow;
Before my wrath 'twill quake!   Sooth then
    will I
No longer fret with toil; unending store
Of riches others shall amass for me.
Mime, the daring, is a king at last;
Lord of the gnomes and ruler of the earth!
A joyous thought that, Mime; who'd have
    guessed
That thou wouldst rise so high?'   Meanwhile
    Siegfried
Was hammering his sword.   At length he cried:
'O Needful, Needful, notablest of swords!
Once again art thou fitted in thine hilt!
In pieces wert thou; I have made thee whole;
No blow can now destroy thee.   If thy strength
Failed at the moment of the father's death,
The son's young life hath fashioned thee anew;

Thy light gleam smiles on him, thy razor-edge
Shall cut deep for him.   Needful ! ever young
To life I have awoke thee.   Dead wast thou
In fragments shattered ; now defiant strength
Gleams from thee.   Show that glorious sheen of
    thine
To all the chaffering herd : cut down the false !
Lay low the villains !   Mime, look thou here !
Thus cuts the sword of Siegfried ! ' So he spake,
And with a mighty stroke he swung the sword
Down on the anvil.   Then the iron mass
Split in two pieces, with an awful din.
And Mime, terrified, fell to the ground
And lay there as one dead.   But Siegfried
    laughed,
And swung aloft his bright undinted blade.

ACT II

DEEP in the forest, where the gaping mouth
Of a great cave yawned black against the trees,
Stood Alberich, in meditation sunk.
' Throughout,' said he, ' the long dark woodland
    night
Before Hate-cavern I have kept my watch,
With ears keen pricked and peering eyes a-
    stretch.
Momentous day ! Art come ? Art glimmering
Athwart the gloom ? what is yon glittering
    gleam ?
Nearer and nearer comes the bright, clear glow ;
Like some ethereal steed it cleaves the brake !
Is this the dragon's conqueror ? Is it now
The hour of Fafner's death ? Th' effulgence
    fades ;
The glow dies down ; the night falls dark again—
Yet who approacheth through the flickering
    shades ? '
Then from the wood's dark fringe spoke
    Wanderer :

'Towards Hate-cavern I have fared by night;
Who doth confront me?' From the rifting clouds
The moon shone out, and lit up Wotan's form.
And Alberich was ware of his dread foe,
And cried: 'Is't thou? What wouldst thou
    here? Away!
Thou shameless thief!' Then Wanderer replied:
'What dost thou here, black Alberich? Dost
    guard
The abode of Fafner?' Loud cried Alberich:
'What mischief hast thou scented hereabouts?
Here tarry not; avaunt! The place hath drunk
The cup of thy deceptions to the dregs!
Wherefore, thou scoundrel, let us live in peace!'
'To watch came I,' said Wanderer, 'not to work;
Who'll bar my path?' Maliciously the dwarf
Laughed, saying: 'Ay, we know thy plotting
    ways!
Were I as dull as in those olden days
When by thy wiles thou took'st me, easily
Again the ring thou mightest rob from me!
Beware! thy cunning well I understand,
Nor is thy weakness hidden from my mind.
With my possessions hast thou paid thy debts;
My ring was given as reward to them
Who built thy burg for thee. The compact made

'Twixt thee and those immense artificers
The runes upon thy spear do testify.
Nor wouldst thou dare to take away again
The price paid to the giants; thou thyself
Wouldst thus destroy thy spear; its lordly shaft,
Strong though it be, would split as doth a straw.'
Him Wotan answered : 'Thou to me wert bound,
Wastrel, by no pact written on the spear :
By strength alone it bent thee to my will,
And with me to the fight it goes again.'
Then Alberich said : 'How proudly dost thou
    boast,
And yet how anxious is thy soul! My curse
Dooms Fafner, guardian of the hoard, to death ;
Who shall inherit ? Shall the envied gold
Again become the Nibelung's property ?
That sears thy soul with sorrow ! If again
I get it in my fist I 'll use the ring
In ways unknown to those dull giant-men !
Then tremble, high protector of the great !
Valhalla's heights I 'll storm with Hell's array,
And hold the world in thrall !' Then Wotan said :
'I know thy scheme, but not to my distress :
Who wins the ring will rule.' Then Alberich :
'In what dark sayings thou dost wrap the truth !
Thy mightiness, I trow, thinks of the breed

Of heroes sprung from thine heroic blood :
I wis thou hast bred up a boy to pluck
The fruit thou dost not dare to steal thyself!'
'With Mime shouldst thou quarrel, not with me,'
Replied lord Wotan ; 'danger lurks with him :
Hither a boy he's bringing, who shall slay
Dread Fafner for him. Naught of me he knows ;
The dwarf doth use the boy for his own ends.
Therefore, my friend, do what is in thine heart !
Yet list thou to my words : Be on thy guard ;
Though nothing of the ring the boy hath heard,
Mime will soon instruct him.'   Alberich
Asked Wanderer : 'And wilt thou stay thine
      hand
From fingering the hoard ?'   And Wotan said :
' Him whom I love I leave to his own skill,
Whether to stand or fall ; he is alone ;
Heroes alone can help me to my rest.'
Then Alberich : 'And shall I have to fight
With Mime only for the magic ring ?'
And Wotan answered : 'Others there are none,
Beside you twain, who covet its delights.'
'Then shall I not possess it ?' asked the dwarf.
Then Wotan said : ' A hero comes to free
The hoard two gnomes are striving to possess.
Fafner, who guards the ring, will meet his death,

And he who takes the ring will own the world.
What wouldst thou more? There dwells the
 dragon-beast,
Warn him that death is nigh, doubtless the hoop
In gratitude he 'll leave thee. Gladly I
Will wake him up for thee. Ho! Fafner, there!
Awake, thou dragon!' Then said Alberich:
'What doth the madman mean? Will it belong
In very truth to me?' From out the cave
Came Fafner's voice: 'Who waketh me from
 sleep?'
And Wotan said: 'A messenger is come
With pressing news for thee; thy life he 'll
 give
For what thou guardest, and thy life beside.'
'What doth he want?' yawned Fafner. Alberich
Cried loud: 'Wake up, thou dragon! Fafner,
 wake!
A mighty hero cometh, who hath sworn
To have thy life.' Then slowly Fafner said:
'I hunger for him.' Wotan made reply:
'Bold is the boy and cunning; sharp his sword!'
And Alberich cried eagerly: 'The ring
He coveteth alone; give it to me
And thus avert the strife; the hoard thou 'lt
 keep,

And live long days in peace!'   Then Fafner
   yawned,
And growled: 'I'm in possession; let me sleep.'
Then laughed lord Wotan, crying: 'Alberich!
That master-stroke hath failed! Wherefore, thou
   knave,
Be chary of thy curses! There's one thing
That I would tell thee; think thou well on it,
All things are bound by rules, which separate
Like from unlike: that law thou canst not change.
I leave thee dominant; stand fast and firm!
'Twere best to fight with Mime; blunders made
Against thy kind will prove least dangerous.
That there are things undreamed of by thy breed
Thou soon shalt learn!'   He spake, and dis-
   appeared
Amid the trees; and stormwinds rose and died.
And Alberich beheld the god depart
With angry eyes, and said: 'He rides away
Upon his lightning-steed, and leaves behind
Sorrow and scorn for me. Ay, laugh away,
Thou greedy, wanton god-gang! I shall see
The day when ye shall all be blotted out!
So long as in the light the gold doth gleam
A cunning watch I'll keep. Their haughtiness
Will prove their own undoing.'   Now the dawn

Shone in the east, and Alberich made haste
To hide him in a hollow in the rocks.
And as the day broke, Mime and Siegfried
Drew near the cave; and Siegfried wore his
    sword.
Then Mime said: ' This is the place ; stop here ! '
And Siegfried sate him down beneath a lime,
And said : ' Here shall I learn the way to fear?
Far hast thou led me ; all the dreary night
Through forest-tracks we've wandered on and on.
Henceforth we twain must part ; if here I fail
To learn what I must learn, alone I'll fare
Forth in the world, of thee for ever free ! '
Then Mime answered : ' Trust me, my dear
    child !
If here, to-day, thou dost not learn to fear,
Elsewhere, another day, 'twere hardly learned !
Dost yonder see the yawning cavern's mouth?
There a fierce, cruel dragon hath his lair ;
Savage and huge beyond all words is he ;
His mouth's a thing of wonder ; hide and hair
Thee at one bolt the beast could put away.'
And Siegfried said : ' 'Twere best to stop his
    mouth ;
Then I should find no danger in his bite.'
And Mime answered : ' Poisoned slaver flows

Forth from his jaws, and whom the spittle's
    spume
Toucheth doth dwindle, flesh and bones, to death.'
' I 'll rush upon his flank,' replied Siegfried,
' And so avoid the searing slaver's bale.'
And Mime went on : ' But a serpent-tail
Waves round about him; whom therewith he
    strikes
And tightly hugs hath no more any limbs.'
And Siegfried said : ' I 'll keep my eye on him,
And so ward off the tail-stroke.   Tell me this :
Hath this great beast a heart ? '   And Mime said :
' A hard and cruel heart ! '   Siegfried went on :
' It beats, belike, where every heart doth beat,
Be it a man's or beast's ? '   And Mime said :
' I wis, my lad; the dragon keeps it there :
Dost thou begin to feel a little fear ? '
Then Siegfried answered : ' In the dragon's heart
Needful I 'll plunge ; is that what men call
    fear ?
Say, gaffer, canst thou teach me nothing more ?
If so, then go thy ways ; I see that here
To fear I shall not learn.'   Then Mime cried :
' O, wait awhile !   Thou thinkest what I said
But windy noise ; thyself must see and hear ;
And then thy senses will forsake thee, sure !

When thy sight swims, the earth beneath thee
    shakes,
And in thy breast thy heart throbs painfully,
Then thou 'lt be grateful that I led thee here
And know the strength of Mime's love for thee.'
Then Siegfried sprang on to his feet, and cried:
'Thou shalt not love me! I have told thee oft!
Get from my sight, and let me be alone.
If thou dost talk of love I 'll leave the place;
I swear it! O, whenever shall I see
The end of all thy hateful knuckling nods
And eyelid-blinkings?   When shall I be quit
Of this old fool?'   And Mime answered him:
'I am about to leave thee; at the spring
I shall be found.   But do thou tarry here,
And when the sun is high be on thy guard.
Hither the dragon from his cave will pass
Upon his way to drink.'   And Siegfried laughed,
And said: 'Yes, Mime, wait thou by the spring;
I 'll let the dragon lap thee up, and then
Needful shall probe his guts!   Therefore beware
Of resting by the fountain; go away
As far as e'er thou canst, and let me be.'
And Mime answered: 'Wilt not come to me
After the struggle?   I could make thee well
If haply thou wast hurt.   And call for me

Shouldst thou need counsel, or when thou hast
    learned
What fear is.' Siegfried waved the dwarf away,
And towards the wood he hobbled, muttering :
'Siegfried and Fafner, Fafner and Siegfried :
Would they might kill each other!' Then
    Siegfried
Sate down again beneath the spreading lime,
And said : 'How glad my heart within me feels
That he is not my father! Woodland scents
Smell sweet for the first time ; the merry day
Hath got a merrier face ; for that sad knave
Is gone, and I shall never see him more.'
Awhile he sate in thought, and then he spake :
'What was my father like ? The same as me,
I wis ; for if friend Mime had a son
He would be just like Mime ? Just as small
And hideous and crookèd-back'd and hunched ?
With halting gait and drooping ears and eyes
Perpetually blear ? The nasty wretch !
I hope I 'll ne'er set eyes on him again.'
He leant back 'gainst the tree, and through the
    leaves
Watched the light flicker. Long he spake no
    word ;
No sound was there beside the forest hum.

At length he spake : 'What was my mother
    like ?
I wonder ; how I wonder ! I can't tell.
I think her eyes were like a roe-deer's eyes,
Only more beautiful. . . . Why did she die
When I was born ?   Do mothers always die
When men are born ?   How awful if 'tis so !
Ah ! would that I could see her !   I, her son !
My mother !   Thou who wast a man's true love !'
He sighed, and stretched his limbs upon the
    sward.
Long time he lay there silent, but the birds
Filled all the thicket with their harmonies.
And presently the boy sate listening
To what a bird was singing overhead.
' Never till now,' he cried, ' sweet little bird,
Have I thy raptures heard; dost make thy
    home
Here in the forest ?   O that I could know
The meaning of thy song !   Perchance it tells
Something of my dear mother.   Mime said
That one might learn to understand the songs
Of all the birds; I would I knew the way !'
So spake Siegfried ; and suddenly his eyes
Lit on a clump of reeds anigh the lime.
' Ha ! I 'll attempt it !   I 'll sing after him,

And tune the reed to copy all his notes!
I do not know his meaning, but I 'll sing
His melody, and so perhaps I 'll learn
Its hidden sense.'   Then Siegfried took his
    sword
And cut a reed, and made a pipe therefrom.
' He stops to listen ; now to my assay ! '
So spake Siegfried, and tried to imitate
The shrill song of the bird.   In vain ; the pipe
Gave back no semblance of the living voice.
Then sadly said Siegfried : ' That sounds not
    right ;
This reed can never catch the subtle song.
Dear little bird, methinks I shall remain
A simple fellow always ; yet 'tis hard
To learn thy lesson.   I am put to shame
By yonder tiny listener ; down he peeps
And cannot hear a note.   Heigho ! I 'll blow
A blast upon my horn ; the silly reed
Is useless.   Now a wood-call thou shalt hear,
A merry one, such as I love to wind.
A while ago I sounded it to lure
A mate to me ; but nothing better came
Than wolves and bears.   Again I 'll try, and see
Whom it may lure me : would that it might
    bring

D

A loving mate !'   He wound his silver horn.
Then through the bushes passed a shivering,
And Fafner crawled from out the wooded shades.
Right up the dell went he, and on a knoll
Stopped with a grinning growl.   Then Siegfried
    turned
And saw the dragon crouching there, and laughed,
And said : ' At last my song hath brought to me
Something to love ; truly a fine mate, thou !'
Then Fafner said : ' Who art thou ?'   Siegfried
    cried :
' Heigho !   Thou art a beast, then, that can talk ?
There's something thou canst tell me.   I am one
Who knows not fear ; pray, wilt thou teach it
    me ?'
Then Fafner said : ' Methinks thou 'rt over bold.'
And Siegfried answered : ' Bold or over bold—
I neither know nor care !   But in good sooth
I 'll kill thee if thou wilt not teach me fear !'
Then Fafner laughed an evil laugh, and said :
' I came to drink, and now I 've found a meal !'
He opened his great maw, and showed his fangs.
Then Siegfried said : ' That is a pretty show !
How thy teeth glisten in their dainty rows !
And yet perhaps 'twere best to shut thy jaws ,
Thy mouth is too wide open.'   Fafner snarled :

' Yea, for vain talk, but not for eating thee ! '
And lashed his tail in fury.   Siegfried cried :
' Oho! thou cruel knave ! 'Twere wrong, me-
    thinks,
To let thee eat me; far the better plan
Would be that I should slay thee empty here.'
Then Fafner bellowed : 'Bah! thou boastful
    cub !
Assay it !'   Siegfried drew his sword and cried :
' Now guard thee, roarer, for the boaster comes !'
So spake Siegfried, and faced the savage beast.
And Fafner crept still higher up the knoll,
And from his nostrils shot forth poisoned breath.
But Siegfried leaped aside, and when the beast
Curled up his tail to seize him, with a bound
He sprang across the dragon's back ; but still
The great tail followed him.   Quick then the
    sword
Flashed in the air and fell ; the dragon shrieked
And heaved his body up, as though to fall
Prone on the boy to crush him ; and his breast
Was now no longer hidden.   To the hilt
Needful went quivering into his heart.
Higher yet reared the dragon in his pain,
Then down he sank upon the bloody sword.
And Siegfried sprang aside, and said to him :

' Lie there, thou hateful beast !   My blade hath
  found
The way to reach thine heart.'   And Fafner asked,
With faint weak voice : ' Who art thou, mighty
  youth,
Who thus hast pierced my heart ?   Who stirred
  thy mind
To do this murderous deed ? '   And Siegfried
  said :
' Much knowledge do I lack ; I do not know
E'en who I am : but thou didst goad me on
To fight thee to the death.'   Fafner replied :
' Thou bright-eyed boy, who dost not know thy-
  self,
I 'll tell thee whom thou 'st slain.   Of giant stock
There were two brothers, Fafner and Fasolt,
Who once ruled o'er the world.   Now both are
  dead.
To gain the cursèd gold I slew Fasolt—
The gold the gods had given ; dragon-shaped,
I, Fafner, last of all earth's giant men,
Kept watch and ward before the gold, and now
A ruddy boy hath slain me.   Hear my words,
Thou winsome youth !   Deceit and treachery
Dog the unhappy master of the hoard ;
And he who urged thee to this cruel deed

Plots death untimely for thee.' Then he gasped:
'Mark well the end, and think upon my words!'
And Siegfried said: 'But tell me whence I
    sprung;
Wise dost thou seem, great dragon, in thy death:
My name will help thee to it; 'tis Siegfried.'
And Fafner sighed, 'Siegfried!' and heaved him-
    self
Upwards a little; then fell back and died.
Then Siegfried said: 'The dead can teach me
    naught:
Be thou my guide, dear Needful!' And laid hold
Of the sword-hilt, and drew it from the wound.
Now in the act blood fell upon his hand;
And Siegfried flinched and cried: 'It burns like
    fire!'
And put his finger in his mouth, and sucked
The bright stain from it. Thoughtfully he stared
Into the distant shades; but suddenly
His ears were startled by a wood-bird's song,
And eagerly he fell a-listening.
At length he spake: 'Doth it not seem as though
Yon bird were speaking to me? All his words
Are plain enow: it must have been the blood
That made me understand them: hark, he sings!'
Thus in the lime the little wood-bird sang:

'To Siegfried now belongs the Nibelung's hoard;
Deep in the cavern he shall find it stored.
If he the Tarnhelm likewise should possess,
'Twill bend to him the nations' haughtiness;
But if he can obtain the magic ring,
'Twill give him power beyond imagining!'
And Siegfried said: 'I thank thee, sweetest bird,
For this thy counsel.' Then towards the cave
He strode forthwith, and vanished in its depths.
Now Mime, glancing fearfully around,
Slunk to the cavern. Quickly Alberich
Slipped from his cleft and barred his path, and
        said:
'Whither art slinking, sly and slippery scamp?'
And Mime cried: 'Is't thou, accursèd one?
I do not need thee here! Why art thou come?'
And Alberich said: 'Dost hunger for my gold?
Art lusting after goods that are not thine?'
Mime made answer: 'Leave the place to me!
This is my haunt; what business hast thou here?'
And Alberich said: 'My business is to watch
Thy secret ploys.' Then Mime made reply:
'What I have planned with toil I will not lose.'
And Alberich answered: 'Was it thou didst win
The ring from father Rhine? Didst thou im-
        plant

Its magic in the hoop?'   Then Mime said:
'Who made the Tarnhelm, which can change all
    forms?
Perchance thou knowest him who needed it?'
And Alberich cried: 'Thou fool! thine ignorance
Was turned to cunning by my magic ring!'
Then Mime said: 'Where is this ring of thine?
The giants took it from thee.   Now thy loss
My craftiness shall win me.'   Alberich
Cried out: 'The niggard steals another's toil!
It is not thine; it is the hero-boy's!'
And Mime said: 'I reared him from a child:
This is my recompense for years of care.
Long have I waited for some small reward
Of all my thought and labour!'   Alberich
Cried angrily: 'So for a bantling's keep
Thou dost demand a kingdom?   Greedy knave!
A mangy dog hath got a better right
Than thou to have the ring!   Thou rogue!   The
    charm
Shall ne'er be thine, I swear it!'   Mime said:
'Then thou shalt have the ring; I'll give it up
If thou wilt call me brother!   The Tarnhelm—
'Tis but a toy—I'd like to have myself:
But both of us can use it.   Let this be
Our sharing of the booty.'   'Share with thee?'

Cried Alberich; 'And share the Tarnhelm too?
How sly thou art! I 'd never sleep a wink
For poring over plots!' Then Mime cried:
'Wilt thou not bargain? Wilt thou give me
    naught?
Am I to go as empty as I came?'
And Alberich made answer: 'Not a nail
Shalt thou divide.' Then Mime in his rage
Cried furiously: 'Then neither ring nor helm
Shall e'er be thine! Against thee I will call
Siegfried and Siegfried's sword; then, brother
    mine,
Be on thy guard!' And Alberich replied:
'Hither from out the cavern doth he come.
Ay, and he hath the Tarnhelm!' Mime said:
'And the ring too!' 'A curse,' cried Alberich,
'Upon him and his ring!' Then Mime laughed,
And said: 'Now thou canst make him give it
    up!
Unless I get it first.' Therewith he turned
And went into the wood. And Alberich,
Muttering, 'The ring is his who gets the ring,'
Stole to his cranny set amid the rocks.
Now Siegfried bare the Tarnhelm and the ring
Forth from the cave, and, looking on them,
    said:

'How ye shall help me I am ignorant;
To take you I was counselled.   Let your gleam
Bear witness of this day, on which I slew
Fafner, yet learned not what is meant by fear.'
Then on his finger Siegfried put the ring,
And in his belt the Tarnhelm.   Suddenly
The wood-bird in the lime-tree sang again:
'Tarnhelm and ring are Siegfried's.   Let his
    heart
Doubt all that Mime saith: the traitor's part
The dragon's blood discloseth.'   Muttering,
Mime came nigh: 'He broodeth o'er his loot:
Hath the wise Wanderer counselled him again?
Sly, doubly sly, must be the dwarf this day;
I must employ my cunning'st artifice
To trap with words this bold, defiant boy!
Hail, Siegfried!   Tell me, hast thou learned to
    fear?'
And Siegfried answered him: 'I have not found
A teacher.'   Mime went on: 'But the beast?
Hast thou then slain him?   Troth he was a mate
Of very evil sort.'   Then said Siegfried:
'Savagely grim and vengeful though he were,
His death yet grieves me, in that worse than he
Still flourish on the earth.   I hate him more
Who made me kill him than I hate the beast.'

Then Mime said : 'Have patience; not for long
Shalt thou behold me; soon eternal sleep
Shall close thine eyes!   The task I gave to thee
Thou hast fulfilled; the booty now I'll take:
Methinks I shall obtain it easily;
For 'tis not hard to fool thee!'   Siegfried asked:
'So thou dost plot my death?'   Mime replied:
'Did I say so?   Hark to me, Siegfried boy:
I hate thee and thy kind; for love of thee
I did not bring thee up; my toil was aimed
To get the hoard and ring.   If now, my son,
Thou wilt not give them up, 'tis very plain
That I must have thy life.'   Then Siegfried said:
'That thou dost hate me I am very glad:
But must thou slay me?'   Mime answered him:
'I said not so: thou dost not understand.
See, thou art weary after all thy toil;
Thy body is afire; to quicken thee
I've brought a wondrous drink.   Whilst thou
     didst weld
Thy sword I brewed the herbs; so drink it up,
And let me get thy sword and then the ring.'
He chuckled grimly.   Siegfried answered him:
'So thou dost want to rob me of my sword
As well as all its winnings!'   Mime cried:
'How thou dost misinterpret!   I have tried

To hide my secret meaning, but in vain!
The stupid booby gets my thoughts all wrong!
Open thine ears, and try to understand;
This is what Mime means: Drink thou thy fill!
Oft has my drink refreshed thee; even when
Thou wast in sullen and unfriendly mood
Thou didst not scorn the cup.' And Siegfried
    said:
' A good drink would I take most willingly:
But how is this one brewed?' Then Mime said:
'Drink it down quick, and have some faith in
    me!
Soon will thy senses fade in night and cloud;
Mindless and motionless thy limbs shall lie.
Then I shall take and hide the precious gold;
And yet, if thou shouldst wake, not e'en the
    ring
Should keep me scatheless from thee. With the
    sword
That thou hast made so sharp for thine own self
I'll hew thine head from off thee; thus at length
I shall possess the ring, and be at rest.'
Again he chuckled grimly. Siegfried said:
'Whilst I am sleeping thou wilt murder me?'
And Mime answered: ' Did I tell thee that?
I only want to chop thine head off, child!

For if I did not hate thee half so well,
Nor had no tale of insults to avenge,
Still I must move thee from mine upward path.
How else should I be master of the hoard
Which Alberich still covets ?   Volsung, drink !
Drink, son of wolves ! and pass down to thy
        death ;
The draught shall be thy last !'   He spake, and
        pressed
The drinking-horn on Siegfried.   Then the boy
Lifted his sword, and cleft the dwarf in twain.
And Alberich was 'ware thereof, and laughed.
'Taste thou my sword, vile babbler !' cried
        Siegfried ;
' Needful hath taken toll of thy contempt :
For this I forged him.'   Thus he spake, and seized
The body of the dwarf, and to the cave
Dragged it, then threw it far into the depths.
' Bide by the hoard !' he cried ; ' with stratagem
Thou didst essay to gain it ; rule it now !
A right good watch-dog will I leave with thee,
To make thee safe from thieves.'   He spake, and
        placed
The dragon's carcass in the cavern's mouth.
' Lie there thou, too, thou gloomy dragon-beast !
Guard the bright treasure with my greedy foe :

So shall ye twain find peace!' Thus Siegfried
    left
The cave, and fell to musing. 'O, the heat
Of all this labour! How the racing blood
Boils in my veins! my hand burns on my brow.
The sun is high; from out the dancing blue
His eye strikes on me fiercely; 'neath the lime
Perchance I shall find shady, cooling rest.'
So saying, Siegfried lay down 'neath the lime.
At length he spake: 'Once more, sweet little
    bird,
I prithee sing, for long hast thou been mute.
I see thee hovering amid the boughs,
I watch thy brethren twittering round thee fly,
Who art so lovely, and who art so loved.
While I—I am so lonely; I have none
To call me kin: my mother died; my sire
Was slain in battle: neither saw their son!
My only comrade was a loathly dwarf
To whom love could not bind me; treacherous
Devices he imagined; him I slew.
Dear little bird, I ask a boon of thee:
Find me a loving mate! So oft I've tried,
And never found one; thou mightst know the
    way.
Give me thy counsel; sing, I'm listening!'

Then sang the bird: 'Now Mime's wicked life
Ended, for Siegfried waits his destined wife.
Upon the high cold fell Brunhilde sleeps:
Around her fire, undying, vigil keeps:
If Siegfried through the flaming barrier strove,
Brunhilde would be his in life and love!'
Then cried Siegfried: 'O loveliest of songs!
O sweetest inspiration!   Its intent
Hath burned into my heart!   My soul's afire
With palpitating longings!   What doth rage
Through heart and sense alike?   Tell me, sweet
        friend!'
Then sang the wood-bird: ''Tis of love I sing,
The bitter sweet so dear to everything:
Passion and grief are woven in the song;
But hungry souls in vain shall never long.'
Then cried Siegfried: 'Exulting I will fare
Forth from the forest towards the rocky fell:
Tell me once more, dear songster, shall I pass
The barrier of flame?   Shall I awake
The sleeping bride?'   The wood-bird sang again:
'No coward shall come nigh the flaming throne;
But only he who fear hath never known.'
Then in delight laughed Siegfried, crying out:
'The stupid boy who hath not learned to fear!
Dear bird, that is myself!   This very day

I vainly tried to learn from Fafner fear.
Now by Brunhilde fain would I be taught ;
But how to find the fell ? '   Thereat the bird
Flew from the tree, and, fluttering, led the way.
Then from Siegfried went up a joyous shout :
' Ay, thou shalt lead the way ; where thou
    dost go
I 'll follow on thy flight ! '   And thus the twain,
The hero and the bird, were lost to sight.

ACT III

'Twas night; the wind howled dismally; a storm
Lit up the crags along the mountain top
And filled the air with thunder.   Wotan stood
Before a gravelike hollow in the rocks.
' Erda,' he cried, ' awake !   From sleep prolonged
I come to rouse thee : rise from out the tomb !
Woman eternal, from thy gloomy depths
Rise to the world above !   O thou who know'st
The wisdom of the ages, Erda, wake !'
Then suddenly the hollow glowed with light;
In a blue mist rose Erda from the depths.
Covered with rime seemed she ; her clothes and
          hair
Glittered with steely brightness.   Then she said :
' A powerful voice hath called me; magic strength
Hath woken me from sleep; who troubleth me ? '
And Wotan said : ' I am the summoner ;
I tried to burst thy shackling bonds of sleep.
I 've roved the world for knowledge; but there
          lives
No one so wise as thou ; for known to thee

Are all things hidden in the depths beneath,
And all that on the mountains, in the vales,
And in the air and in the waters move.
Thy breath's the breath of life; where thought
    is born
Thy soul doth brood; and all to thee is plain.
To have thy counsel did I waken thee.'
Then Erda said: 'My sleep is but a dream,
My dreams are thoughts, and wisdom is but
    thought.
And when I sleep the Nornir keep their watch;
Weaving their rope, they weave in all I dream:
Why dost not ask the Nornir?' Wotan said:
'In the world's grip the Nornir watch and weave;
What is and is to be they cannot change.
Thy wisdom only could my quest avail;
How best to stop an ever-rolling wheel?'
Erda made answer: 'All the works of men
I dimly understand. A hero once
Subdued me to his will; a Wish-Maiden
I bore to Wotan, whom he taught to call
His bands of heroes to him. Bold is she
And wise withal; why hast thou woken me
Instead of seeking Wotan's child and mine?'
Then said the Wanderer: 'Meanest thou the
    maid

E

Brunhilde, the Valkyrie? She hath spurned
The ordinance of him who rules the storms:
That which the lord of battles fain had done
But sware he would not, though it pained him
    sore,
The girl made bold to do against his will.
The Father of the Fights hath punished her;
Her eyes are closed, and on the rugged fell
She sleeps her long deep sleep. She will awake
Only to be the plaything of a man.
What boots it, then, for me to question her?'
For long was Erda silent, then she spake:
'Weak and confused am I since I awoke;
The world seems wild and strange. The Valkyrie,
The witch's child, doth pine in bonds of sleep,
E'en as her mother slept! Shall frowardness
Be curbed by him who taught it? Shall the deed
Anger his heart who first instilled the thought?
Doth he who knoweth right and guardeth truth,
Fallen, uphold his rule with broken vows?
O, let me sink beneath again; let sleep
Lock up mine understanding!' Wotan said:
'Thou shalt not yet pass hence; I have the
    power
To hold thee here. Wise Erda, thou hast struck
The sting of care in Wotan's dauntless heart;

His soul is filled with fear of that foul death
Foretold erstwhile by thee, and sorrow holds
His courage in its grip.   If thou, in truth,
Art of all women in the world most wise,
Tell me how best the god may combat care?'
Then Erda cried: 'Thou art not what thou
    seem'st!
Why hast thou broken in upon my peace?
O loose thy magic spell, and set me free!'
And Wotan said: 'Thou art not what thou
    ween'st!
Thine endless wisdom draws towards its end;
Thy knowledge vanisheth at my behest.
Dost know what Wotan willeth?   In thine ear
I call thee the Unwise One, that for aye
Bereft of care thou mayest sleep thy sleep.

   .   .   .   .

The twilight deepeneth fast about the gods;
I feel no anguish, for it is my doom.
What midst the pangs of doubt I did decree
With joy I will fulfil: I lost the world
For hatred of the Nibelung, but love
Hath pointed to the Volsung as my heir.
He whom I chose, who doth not know me yet,
A daring boy, of counsels ignorant,
Did seize the Nibelung's ring: devoid of guile

And filled with love's rejoicing he shall void
The curse that Alberich laid upon the gold.
For fear he doth not know.   He shall awake
Brunhilde, thine own child, and she shall strive
Towards the world's redeeming.   Wherefore
    sleep,
And gloat in dreams upon my speedy death !
Away then, Erda, mother of all fear !
Mother of sorrow !   Get thee to thy sleep
That shall not have an end.'   Then Erda sank
Below the earth, and darkness fell again.
But Wotan leaned against the rocks, to wait
For Siegfried's coming ; and behind the hills
The moon arose.   And presently Siegfried
Drew nigh, and said : ' Where is my little bird ?
With fluttering flight and merry chirping song
He hath beguiled the road, and now he 's gone.
Myself I 'll find the fell ; I 'll roam on still
Along the way we came.'   Then Wotan said :
' Boy, whither goest thou?' And Siegfried cried :
' The voice that hails me will point out the road.
I seek a fell beleaguered round with flame,
Where sleeps a maiden I would fain awake.'
And Wotan said : ' Who bade thee seek the fell,
And filled thy heart with love for her that
    sleeps ? '

Siegfried made answer: ''Twas a singing bird
Who gave me tidings of her.'   Wotan laughed:
'A twittering bird, forsooth!   No mortal man
Can understand their jargon!   How couldst thou
Gather a meaning from a wood-bird's song?'
Then Siegfried said: 'It was a dragon's blood
That worked the miracle—a beast I slew
Without Hate-cavern: hardly had his blood
Touched my tongue-tip before I understood
All that the birds were singing.'   Wotan said:
'Who urged thee on to slay that savage beast?'
Siegfried made answer: 'Mime guided me—
A faithless dwarf who tried to teach me fear;
Yet did the dragon urge me to the stroke
That brought him death, by gaping with his jaws
As though he fain would eat me.'   Wotan asked:
'Who forged the blade that slew so stout a
      foe?'
Siegfried replied: 'I forged the sword myself,
Because the smith could not; else I had been
Swordless to-day.'   Then Wotan asked again:
'But who did forge the splinters of a sword
Which thou didst weld into a sword again?'
'How can I tell?' cried Siegfried; 'all I know
Is that the splinters were no use to me:
I had to start and make the sword afresh.'

'That I know well!' cried Wotan, and he
    laughed.
Then Siegfried cried: 'Why dost thou laugh
    at me?
Old gossip, I must tell thee once for all
I will not stay here chattering!   If the road
Thou canst point out, then do so, but if not,
I prithee hold thy tongue.'   Then Wotan said:
'Softly, my lad!   If thou dost think me old,
Thou shouldst have reverence for me.'   Siegfried
    cried:
'O what a jape!   A fool of an old man
Hath plagued me from my cradle up till now;
But him I've brushed aside.   If thou dost stop
Much longer in my way, beware lest thou
Share Mime's fate!   I cannot see thy face;
What art thou like?   Why dost thou wear a hat
That covers up thy face?'   Then Wotan said:
''Tis Wanderer's habit when he meets the wind.'
Then Siegfried cried: 'And thou hast lost an eye!
Doubtless some traveller who tired of thee
Doth own the trophy!   Get out of my way,
Or haply thou wilt lose the other one!'
Wotan made answer: 'Verily, my son,
Thine ignorance doth stand thee in good stead.
Methinks thine eyes are very like the eye

That's left to me.'   Then Siegfried laughed out
    loud:
'How comical thou art!   Yet hark to me!
I will not stop here fooling; thou must come
And point me out my road, then go thine own.
For naught else do I need thee: dost thou hear?
If so, speak up, or else I'll scatter thee!'
Then Wotan said: 'If thou didst know me, boy,
Thou wouldst not scorn me thus.   For bitterly
Thy threats assail the heart which loves thee so.
Thy race hath ever been beloved of me;
E'en when mine anger wrought it lasting grief:
Rouse not my wrath, then, thou most gallant
    youth,
For fear it should consume both thee and me!'
Then Siegfried cried: 'O thou most stubborn
    wight!
Wilt thou not move?   That is the road, I wis,
That leadeth onward to the sleeping girl;
So said the bird that left me.'   Wotan said:
'It fled to save its life.   The raven's lord
Did bar its path; woe to yon bird, I say,
If he should find it!   And thou shalt not tread
The road thy guide hath pointed out to thee!'
'Oho!' cried Siegfried, 'thou art passing bold!
Who art thou, then, who thus wilt hinder me?'

And Wotan said : 'I guard this mountain fell :
My power holds the maiden in her trance.
Who wakes and wins her hath for ever robbed
My virtue from me.   But a fiery sea
Surges around the maiden ; glowing flames
Lick round the fell ; who would the bride possess
Must face that withering heat.   Lift up thine
        eyes !
Dost see yon light ?   Still higher mounts the
        glare,
The furnace waxes hotter ; burning clouds
And darting fire-tongues wave and wander there.
Already hath the sheen encircled thee ;
Soon will the fire devour thee utterly.
Turn back, rash boy !'   Then Siegfried answered
        him :
'Turn back thyself, thou braggart !   Where the
        flames
Rage fiercest I will go to my Brunhild' !'
Then Wotan barred the pathway with his spear,
And said : 'If fire can breed no fear in thee,
My spear shall hold thee back !   My hand doth
        grasp
The shaft that giveth power ; e'en the sword
That thou didst forge this shaft once brake in
        twain ;

Break it again upon the deathless spear!'
Then Siegfried drew his sword, and cried aloud:
My father's foe! So I have found thee here?
Vengeance is mine at last; swing out thy shaft
That I may make it even as the dust!'
He spake, and rushed on Wotan, and the sword
Hacked till the spear went flying into shreds.
And whilst the roar of thunder filled the air
Wotan shrank backwards, crying, 'Go thy way!
I cannot stop thee!' And upon the storm
The god was carried from the hero's ken.
Then said Siegfried: 'My coward foe hath fled
With damaged weapons. Ha! that heavenly
    glow!
What winsome light is there! A radiant path
Stretches before me! I will bathe in flame,
Therein to find my bride! Oho! Oho!
'Tis merry work this finding of a mate!'
He wound his horn, and plunged into the fire.
Now when Siegfried had crossed the flaming belt,
Unhurt by reason of his fearlessness,
He found himself upon a rocky fell
Where pine-woods whispered to the fickle winds.
And Siegfried said: 'How sweet is solitude
Upon this sunny height! But what lies there
Asleep within the shadow of the wood?

It is a warhorse, tired with many a fray !'
Then Siegfried went towards the sleeping steed,
And suddenly he cried : 'What glittering flash
Of armour blinds mine eyes?   What glorious
    arms
Are these ?   Shall I uplift them ?   Ha ! a man
Lies sleeping ; and his face is fair to see !
His head is weighed down by the heavy helm ;
'Twould ease him did I loosen it.'   He spake,
And took the helmet from the sleeper's head.
Now in the act long curly hair brake forth
And flowed about the face ; and Siegfried cried :
'Ah ! that is lovely ! 'Tis just like the clouds
That fringe with waves the azure of the sky ;
It is as when the sun's enchanting face
Smiles through the clustering tangles of the mist !
His breast is heaving with each long-drawn
    breath ;
Shall I undo his stifling coat of mail ?
Come, Needful, cut the steel !'   Then down both
    sides
The hero cut the corslet and the greaves,
And took them off the sleeper.   There Brunhild'
Lay in the clinging garments of a girl.
And Siegfried cried in wonder: ''Tis no man ! . . .
What spell is laid upon my burning heart ?

What fiery awe hath fastened on mine eyes?
My senses reel and stagger; whom to call
To help me I know not!˜ O mother dear,
Befriend me now!' Thus cried the hero-boy,
And laid his head upon Brunhilde's breast.
Long time he lay thus silent, but at last
He started up and cried: 'What can I do
To wake the maid and see her opened eyes?
Her opened eyes! The very light of them
Would blind me! Dare I face that brilliance?
All things seem waving round me in a mist;
My mind is darkened; fires are burning me;
Both heart and hand are trembling. Is this fear?
O mother mine, alas for thy brave boy!
A sleeping girl hath taught him how to fear!
How can I put an ending to this fear?
How find my courage? Must I wake the maid
That I myself may wake from out this trance?
Sweet tremblings overpower me as I gaze
Upon her rosy lips; her breath so warm
Is fragrant as the flowers! Girl, awake!
She heedeth not. Then, though I die for it,
I'll draw life from those sweetest of all lips!'
He kissed her, with a long and lingering kiss.
Then did Brunhilde slowly wake from sleep,
And, sitting up, she cried: 'Hail! sun and light!

Hail! day that givest joy! My sleep was long,
But now I am awake. How hight the man
Who hath awakened me?' Then Siegfried said:
''Twas I who crossed the fire that girds the fell;
'Twas I who took the helmet from thine head:
I did awake thee, and my name's Siegfried.'
Then cried Brunhilde: 'Hail to ye, great gods!
Hail, world! Hail, glittering earth! my sleep is
    done,
Siegfried awoke me, and I am awake—'
And Siegfried said: 'Hail, mother! Hail, thou
    earth
Life nourishing, that I should see those eyes
Streaming their glories on me!' Then Brunhild':
'Thou that didst bear him, hail! Hail to the
    earth
Who nourished him! His glance alone could
    break
The endlessness of sleep—Siegfried, Siegfried!
Immortal hero, wakener of my life,
Conquering light! Didst know, thou world-
    beloved,
How I did love thee? Thou wast in my
    thoughts
Unceasingly, my constant care wast thou!
I cherished thee before thy limbs were formed;

Before thy birth my shield did shelter thee :
So long ago I loved thee, dear Siegfried !'
Then Siegfried asked : ' My mother did not die ?
She only fell asleep ? '   Brunhilde said :
' Dear boy, thy mother never will come back—
Thyself am I, if thy pure heart can love.
What thou dost lack my wisdom can supply,
For I am wise, because I love thee so.
O Siegfried, Siegfried ! conquering light ! my
    love
Hath been thine always ; for to me alone
Was Wotan's purpose plain.   My guiding thought
I never told, nor pondered, only felt—
It drove me on to battle and to toil ;
It nerved me to defy the dreadful god
Who prompted it ; for it I suffered ; sleep
Laid chains on me, because it was a thought
I could not utter.   Canst thou guess that
    thought ?
'Twas love for thee.'   Then Siegfried answered
    her :
' Thy words are sweet ; and yet my mind is
    dark—
I watch the brilliance of thy gleaming eyes ;
I feel the warm glow of thy scented breath ;
I hunger for the soft notes of thy voice ;

And yet thy meaning is not plain to me—
I cannot understand what is not nigh;
For all my mind is centred in thyself—
With timid fear thou 'st fettered me; alone
Of mortals hast thou taught me cowardice.
In bonds unbreakable I 'm bound, do thou
Give back to me the courage that was mine!'
Brunhilde looked beyond him to the wood,
And said: 'There is my Grane, faithful horse!
How gaily he is feeding—he who slept
So long near me, till Siegfried woke us both.'
And Siegfried answered her: 'Mine eyes do
        feast
Upon thy glorious lips; a burning thirst
Possesses mine, which only thine can quench!'
Brunhilde pointed with her hand, and said:
'There lies the shield that heroes did protect;
I see the helmet that did guard my head:
Yet they shall shield and cover me no more!'
And Siegfried said: 'A girl hath pierced mine
        heart;
A woman hath destroyed me; for I came
With neither shield nor helm!'   Brunhilde said:
'I see my gleaming corslet; a sharp sword
Slit it in two; the maiden's guard is gone;
Unarmed and helpless I am but a girl!'

Then Siegfried cried: 'Through burning fires I
    strove
To be with thee ; no shield protected me !
The fury of the flames is in my breast ;
The raging of the fire is in my blood ;
Consuming heat doth torture me ; the glow
That shone around the fell where thou didst
    sleep
Is in mine heart ! O quench this burning pain,
Put out this searing fire !' He seized the girl,
With passion strung to madness. But Brunhild'
Wrenched herself free, and cried : 'No god hath
    dared
To touch me ! Heroes left me unassailed !
I left Valhalla pure. Alas ! Alas !
Shame and disgrace await me ; I am wronged
By him who woke me ! He hath ta'en away
My shield and helm : I am myself no more !'
And Siegfried said : 'For me thou art the girl
Who sleepeth still ; thou art not yet awake.
But I would wake thee ; wilt thou be my wife ?'
Brunhilde cried : 'My senses whirl and sway ;
My wisdom falters and my prudence fades !'
Then asked Siegfried: 'Didst thou not sing to
    me
A song wherein thy wisdom was the love

To light my life and thine !'   Brunhilde said :
' Darkness obscures my sight; mine eyes are
    dim ;
The light grows faint ; night hath enveloped me.
From out the clouds of pain strange phantom-
    forms
Rise up against me ; horrors stalk abroad,
Hovering about my path !'   She clasped her
    hands
Over her eyes.   Then Siegfried gently drew
Her hands away, and said : ' Night makes afraid
The eyes that are fast closed ; let in the light,
And all thy haunting ghosts will slink away !
Come out of those dark shadows, and behold
The sun-bright gleam of day !'   Brunhilde cried :
' Sun-bright the day on which I came to shame !
O Siegfried, Siegfried !   Dost thou understand ?
I was and am eternal, and my love
For thee shall be eternal !   Siegfried dear !
Thou treasure of the world, life of the earth !
Thou smiling hero !   Let me, let me go !
Leave me in peace !   Come not so nigh to me
With all thy passion raging in thine eyes !
O, force me not to thine imperious will !
Destroy her not who puts her trust in thee !

.   .   .   .

Hast never seen, in some clear mountain pool,
Thy face reflected?   Did it make thee glad?
Yet when the water ruffled into waves,
And the bright surface of the pool was marred,
Thine image vanished; naught was there to see,
But only ripples riding on and on.
So leave me quiet; trouble not my heart;
And then for ever shall thine image glow
Reflected from my soul!   Siegfried! Siegfried!
Love thine own self, and have no thought for
    me;
Thou wouldst not hurt her who is thine for aye?'
Then cried Siegfried : 'I love thee!   Would that
    thou
Didst love me too!   Myself I have no more,
O would that I had thee!   A glorious flood
Streams on before me; I can only see
Those beauteous waves!   Mine image blotted
    out,
I long to cool my passion in their depths;
O that their waves might swamp my soul with
    bliss!
Awake, Brunhilde!   Live and laugh again!
Sweetest of loves, be mine, be mine, be mine!'
Then said Brunhilde sadly : 'Siegfried! thine?
I have been thine for ever.'   Siegfried cried :

'Then be mine now!' Brunhilde answered him:
'I will be thine for ever.'   Siegfried cried:
'That thou wilt be for ever, be thou now!
Let me enfold thee, let me hold thee fast!
Let my breast beat its love-notes close to thine!
Let eyes meet eyes, and breath go up with
      breath!
Let mouth kiss mouth!   So mine thou truly art,
As thou dost say thou wert and wilt be mine!
So only shall I quench my burning pain.
Brunhilde, say thou lov'st me?'   In his arms
He clasped her.   Then Brunhilde answered him:
'Dost ask if I do love thee?   Godlike peace
Is plunged in tempest; purity in lust;
My heavenly teachings fail me, whirled away
By love's exulting stream!   *If* I am thine!
O Siegfried, Siegfried!   Hast thou watched my
      face?
Mine eyes devour thee; and thou art not blind?
Mine arms enfold thee; and thou dost not burn?
My blood doth surge against thee; and its fire
Thou dost not feel?   O Siegfried, art afraid
Of this wild girl of thine?'   Then Siegfried
      cried:
'Now are the currents of our blood aflame!
Our eyes devour each other; arms entwined

Throb longingly !   My courage is come back,
And that same fear that I could never learn—
Which even thou couldst hardly make me know—
I, like a fool, have clean forgot again ! '
Then laughed Brunhilde in love's ecstasy :
' My hero-boy ! who art the lord of men !
Thou pride of them who wrought the world's
    best deeds !
Gladly I love thee ; gladly yield to thee ;
Gladly with thee go down to shame and death !
Good-bye, Valhalla, and thy glittering world !
Thy stately burg shall crumble to the dust !
Good-bye, the splendid greatness of the gods !
Thou race eternal, pass away in peace !
Ye Nornir, break your woven rope of runes !
The twilight of the gods begins to fall !
The night of our destruction darkens fast !
Siegfried, my star, lights up the dreary hour ;
For he is mine for ever, mine alone !
He is mine own, mine only one, mine all ;
The love that lighteth us hath laughed at death ! '
Then Siegfried cried : ' My darling is awake
And smiles at me !   Brunhilde lives again !
Hail, sun, that shines upon us !   Hail, thou day
That on our love hath dawned !   Hail, glorious
    light,

That hath the bonds of night asunder burst!
Hail, world, that with Brunhilde wakes once
    more!
She is awake, she lives, she smiles at me!
My star, Brunhilde, lighteth up the world!
For she is mine for ever, mine alone!
She is mine own, mine only one, mine all;
The love that lighteth us hath laughed at death!'

THE TWILIGHT OF THE GODS

THE TWILIGHT OF THE GODS

PRELUDE

'Twas night, and on the summit of the fell
Brunhilde's fire still burned.   Beneath the pines
Sate the three Nornir, weavers of the fates,
Tall sisters clad in long and dark array.
At length the eldest sister spake and said :
' What light is there ? '   The second Norn went
    on :
' Doth the day break ? '   The youngest sister
    said :
' 'Tis Loge's host still ravening round the fell.
The night is young ; come, let us spin and sing ! '
Then said the second sister to the first :
' And if we spun and sang, where wouldst thou
    find
A holding for the rope ? '   Her sister rose,
And fastened to the branch of a great pine
Her golden cord, then said : ' For weal, for woe,
Thus fasten I the rope, and thus I sing :

Once did I weave beside the world's ash-tree,
Whose bole was bowered in perpetual green.
In the cool shadows purled a tiny stream,
And wisdom lay within its murmurings.
There sang I mystic songs.   A fearless god
Desired to drink the water and be wise ;
His tribute was an eye.   From the world-ash
Lord Wotan brake a branch, and shaped a shaft
Whereon to fit his spear.   As time went on
The wound spread o'er the wood ; the leaves
     fell down ;
The great tree rotted, and the fountain dried.
Dark was my song with sorrow, and no more
Weave I beside the ash-tree ; gloomy firs
Must hold my rope for me.   Now, sister, sing ;
It is thy turn to weave ! '   Then sang the Norn :
' Truth-counselling runes and bond-compelling
     oaths
Wrote Wotan on his spear-shaft ; sovereignty
O'er all the world was his who held the shaft.
In fight a fearless hero brake the spear ;
There was destroyed the witness of the runes.
Then Wotan called Valhalla's heroes forth
To fell the withered ash-tree of the world.
Down crashed the tree ; at once the brook ran
     dry.

Round a sharp rock I cast the rope for thee ;
Sing, sister, sing ; it is thy turn to weave.'
Then sang the Norn : 'There is a mighty burg
Which giants builded ; gods and heroes throng
Lord Wotan's courts.   Around Valhalla's walls
Great piles of faggots loom towards the sky ;
The ash-tree once were they—when burns the
      wood
With gleaming flame, and rends those princely
      halls,
The twilight of the gods is near at hand.
If this ye know, then twist the rope afresh ;
From northwards do I throw it back to thee ;
Spin, sister, spin, and speak to us in song !'
Then sang the eldest of the sisters three :
'Doth the day break ?   Or doth the fire still
      glow ?
My sight is dim with grief ; the wondrous past
Fades from my memory ; once Loge moved
In lambent fires ; what is become of him ?'
Then sang the second sister : 'He was tamed
By Wotan and the magic of his spear.
Whilst whispering counsels to the god his lord,
He sought to set him free from irksome bonds
By gnawing at the spear-shaft.   With its point
Wotan compelled the shifty god to fence

Brunhilde's fell with flame.'   Then sang the
     Norn,
The youngest of the sisters: 'On a day
Wotan will plunge the fragments of his spear
Deep in the shifty god's bright-glowing breast
Thereat the brands will kindle; them the god
Will hurl upon the looming faggot-piles
That were the world-ash.   Would ye know the
     day
When this shall happen ye must weave again.'
Then said the eldest Norn: 'The long night
     wanes,
And I am tired.   I cannot see the threads;
The rope is all entangled.   Dreamy thoughts
Whirl through my brain; the Rhine gold
     Alberich stole—
Dost know where 'tis?'   Then said the second
     Norn:
'The sharp stone cuts the rope; the threads
     hang limp;
The clue is thin, the weaving is awry.
The Nibelung's ring opposeth me; its curse
Eats to the core of mine unwoven strands.
Canst tell the end?'   The youngest sister said:
'The rope's too slack; it doth not reach to me:
If towards the north I throw the ragged fringe

It must be tighter stretched.'   So on the rope
The Norn pulled heavily, and in the midst
It brake in two.   ' 'Tis broken !' cried the Norn.
' 'Tis broken !' cried her sister.   And again,
' 'Tis broken !' cried the eldest of the three.
Then did the Nornir take the broken strands
And lash themselves together, as they sang :
' Thus ends eternal knowledge !   The world cares
No more for wisdom !   Mother, down to thee
We sink below !'   And thus they disappeared.

.   .   .   .   .   .

Now the sun flamed upon the eastern skies,
And quenched the radiance of Brunhilde's fires.
Together from the cave came forth the twain,
Brunhilde and Siegfried.   Brunhilde led
Her bay horse Grane, and Siegfried was clad
In armour.   Then Brunhilde spake, and said :
' Dear heart, if I refused to let thee go
Forth in the world to do fresh feats of arms
I should not truly love thee.   Yet one fear
Doth make me pause ; dear love, I want to know
That all thine heart is given unto me !
Wisdom, god-taught, I freely gave to thee ;
I made thee master of the sacred runes ;
Yet thou hast robbed me of my maiden strength—
Thou before whom henceforth I bow my head.

My wisdom gone, my love alone remains—
A powerless love : Siegfried, do not despise
Thy poor girl who doth give thee all she hath
Because she hath no more!'   Siegfried replied :
'Loved one, thy gifts outrun my feeble wits;
Chide not if all thy lessons are not learned!
But there is one thing that I understand :
Brunhilde lives for me; 'twas easy learned
To love Brunhilde's image for all time!'
Then said Brunhilde : 'Wouldst thou fan my
        flame
Of love unquenchable, think on thyself
And all that thou hast done ! Think on the fires
That ringed the fell so fearlessly o'erpassed—'
'To win Brunhilde!' cried her lover.   'Think
On her who lay beneath the long steel shield
Whom sleeping thou didst find; whose helm
        thine hands
Did gently take away—'   'To wake Brunhild'!'
Cried Siegfried.   'Think on all our plighted vows
To be forever one ; think on the troth
We sware to one another; think on love
Brightening the brief span of our wedded lives.
Ponder these things, and so thy love for me
Shall never faint nor fade!'   Then said Siegfried :
'Dear one, I leave thee in the hallowing charge

Of glowing flames; but ere I go, this ring
I give to thee in barter for thy runes.
Its virtue was the virtue of my deeds;
A dragon guarded it, and him I slew.
Keep thou the charm in witness of my love !'
Gladly Brunhilde donned the magic ring,
And said : 'There's naught I treasure more than
    this :
Take thou my horse instead ; he used to fly
Bravely across the heavens ; but with me
He lost his magic powers.   Never more
Upon clouds trembling with the thunder-shock
Shall he dash on undaunted.   Yet my steed
Will follow thee wherever thou dost go,
Even through fire, and will not turn aside.
He will obey thee, therefore treat him well ;
He understands thy meaning ; Siegfried, kiss
Dear Grane often for me ! '   Siegfried said :
' Thy strength alone will help me to great deeds !
My battles thou hast chosen ; victory
Will rest with thee ! Upon thy horse's back,
Protected by thy shield, I am no more
Siegfried, but one who doth Brunhilde's will ! '
Then cried Brunhilde : ' Would I were thy soul ! '
And Siegfried said: 'My courage flows from thee.'
Brunhilde answered : ' Then art thou the twain,

Both Siegfried and Brunhilde.'   Siegfried said :
' Where'er I am, there thou art with me too.'
Brunhilde asked him : ' Is the rocky fell
Left desolate ? '   And Siegfried answered her :
' We both are there as one.'   Brunhilde cried :
' O sacred stock, immortal race of gods !
Look graciously upon our love sublime !
Divided, who can part us ?   Separate,
We still are one ! '   Then Siegfried spake and
        said :
' Hail, dear Brunhilde, loadstar of my life !
Hail, thou bright-gleaming stream of love divine ! '
Brunhilde cried : ' Hail, Siegfried dear !   Thou
        light
That conquerest the darkness of my life !
Hail, thou bright-gleaming stream of love divine ! '
Then Siegfried led his horse adown the rocks,
And soon he vanished from Brunhilde's ken.
Yet ever and anon his plaintive horn
Sounded its farewells from the darkening vale,
Until at last Brunhilde stood alone.

ACT I

THE HALL OF THE GIBICHUNGS ON THE RHINE

Now Gunther and Gudrun sate on a throne
Above the salt, and lower down the board
Dotted with drinking vessels, Hagen sate.
Then Gunther spake: 'Hagen, what thinkest
    thou?
Is my dominion stablished o'er the Rhine?
Say, shall my rule be worthy of my race?'
Him Hagen answered: 'Envious am I
Of thy wide-spreading fame; our mother knew
My heart, and bade me curb my jealousy.'
Then Gunther laughed: 'Thou shouldst not
    envy me,
'Tis I who envy thee! If I was heir
To lands and treasure, thou wast dowered with wit.
Half-brothers wrangling never yet have found
A happier way to end their bickering;
For when I question thee about my fame
I praise the keenness of thy subtle wit.'
Then Hagen said: 'I blame my wits that thou

Art not e'en greater than thou art to-day:
For I have heard of wealth the like of which
No man called Gibichung hath ever seen.'
Then Gunther said: ' If thou dost not reveal
This wondrous treasure I shall blame thee too.'
Hagen replied: ' I see the Gibichungs
Strong in the summer beauty of their prime;
And yet thou, Gunther, hast not found a wife;
Thou, Gudrun, hast not chosen out a mate.'
Then Gunther asked him: ' Is there any one
Who would enhance the glories of our stock?'
Hagen made answer: ' In the wide wide world
There is no woman lovelier than her
Whose home lies high upon the rugged fell.
Around her palace surge undying fires,
And only he who vanquisheth the flames
May   woo   Brunhilde.'   Gunther   questioned
      him:
' Dost think my courage would suffice thereto?'
And Hagen said: ' A stronger than thyself
Is destined to possess her.'   Gunther asked:
' How hight the gallant hero?'   Hagen said:
' His name is Siegfried, from the Volsungs sprung.
A twin-born pair, Sieglinde and Siegmund,
Urged on by love begat this mighty son.
His manhood is the manhood of the woods:

I would he were the husband of Gudrun.'
Then Gudrun asked: 'What hath he done so
    bold
To be accounted great among the great?'
Her Hagen answered: 'Once upon a time
A savage dragon watched the Nibelung's hoard
By Hate-cavern.   His gaping maw Siegfried
Shut for all time, and slew him with his sword.
Such deed it was that gave the hero fame.'
Then Gunther said: 'I've heard of this same
    hoard:
Doth it contain a wondrous store of gold?'
Hagen replied: 'Who understands its use
Can rule the world.'   Said Gunther eagerly:
'Hath Siegfried kept it?'   Hagen answered him:
'Yea, verily, the Nibelungs are his slaves.'
'Can only Siegfried woo and win Brunhild'?'
'None other dares to cross the hindering fires.'
Then from his throne rose Gunther, vexed at
    heart:
'Why dost thou waken dogs that sleeping lie?
Dost wish to make me long in impotence
For that which I can never hope to win?'
Said Hagen: 'But if Siegfried brought the girl
Home to thee here, would Brunhild' not be
    thine?'

Then Gunther strode across the hall, and cried :
'What human power could induce the swain
To free his bride for me ?'   And Hagen said :
'Thy prayer would prevail, if first Gudrun
Had woven wiles about the hero's heart.'
Then cried Gudrun : 'I will not hear thee scoff !
Thou wicked Hagen !   Who am I to touch
The heart of Siegfried ?   If in all the world
There is no hero like to him for strength,
The loveliest of women on the earth
Long since hath yielded to his instant love.'
Then Hagen spake : 'Bethink thee of the drink
Kept secret in yon shrine, and put thy trust
In him who brewed it : it will bind to thee
In lover's bonds the hero of thy dreams.
If Siegfried came and drank thereof, a sleep
Would fall upon his mind ; he would forget
That he had ever won a woman's heart,
And picture thee the first love of his youth.
Tell me, what think ye of friend Hagen's plan ?'
Then Gunther, leaning on the table, said :
'Grimhilde, blest be thou, who gav'st to us
Hagen for brother !'   While his sister sighed,
And said : 'I would that I could see Siegfried !'
And Gunther said : 'How shall we find him out ?'
Hagen made answer : 'On adventures bent

The world will soon become too strait for him :
Be sure his restless quest will lead him on
To where old Rhine flows past the Gibichungs.'
'I'll bid him welcome gladly,' Gunther laughed.
Now as he spake a distant horn was heard.
'It soundeth from the river,' Gunther said.
And Hagen went towards the river bank
And shouted back : 'A boat comes up apace,
And in it are a warrior and his horse.
With long, slow stroke, as though he rows at ease,
He drives his skiff against the rushing stream ;
So strong an oarsman surely must be he
Who slew the dragon ; ay, it is Siegfried !'
Then Gunther shouted : 'Is he going past ?'
And Hagen put his two hands to his mouth
And shouted loudly : 'Whither goest thou,
Most mighty hero ?'   Siegfried answered him :
'To see the scion of the Gibichungs.'
Then Hagen cried : 'I bid thee to his halls !
Make fast thy craft ; my lord awaiteth thee !
Hail, Siegfried, mighty hero !'   Now Gudrun
Gazed for a while on Siegfried, while her eyes
Spoke to the thrilling gladness of her heart.
And then she slowly passed within the house.
Then said Siegfried : 'Where is the Gibichung ?'
And Gunther answered : 'I in truth am he.'

'Thy fame is noised abroad beyond the Rhine,'
Said Siegfried : 'wherefore fight me to the death,
Or be my friend.'   Then Gunther answered him :
'Why speak of battles ?   Thou art welcome here.'
And Siegfried asked : 'Where can I put my
      horse ?'
And Hagen answered : 'I will look to him.'
'Thou callest me by name,' the hero said :
'Where hast thou seen me ?'   Hagen made reply :
'I knew thee only by thy wondrous strength.'
Then said Siegfried : 'Treat Grane well for me !
No better horse than he hath ever breathed !'
So Hagen led the charger to the stalls
And fed him there, and presently returned.
Meanwhile lord Gunther spake unto his guest
And said : 'I bid thee welcome to my halls.
Whate'er thou seest is thy very own :
My lands, my peoples, mine inheritance
Are thine ; by mine own body I have sworn
To be thy man.'   Then Siegfried answered him :
'Nor lands nor peoples can I offer thee ;
Nor yet the home that goes from son to son.
My body is my one inheritance,
And that life wears away.   I have a sword,
Self-wrought ; it shall be witness to mine oath
That I am thine.'   Behind them Hagen's voice

Came croaking : ' Rumour saith that thou art lord
Of all the Nibelung's treasure ? '   Siegfried said :
' The treasure had escaped my memory ;
So little do I prize such idle store !
I left it lying in the self-same cave
Wherein a dragon watched it jealously.'
Then Hagen asked : ' Didst thou not take away
Some portion of the booty ? '   Siegfried said :
' I took away this network, knowing not
What use it hath.'   Then Hagen made reply :
' It is the Tarnhelm, cunningest of works
Wrought by the cunning smiths of Nibelheim :
Its virtue is, when on thine head 'tis placed,
To change thy form to any living shape ;
Dost thou desire to visit distant lands ?
Straightway it sets thee down upon their shores.
Hast taken nothing else beside the helm ? '
Then Siegfried said : ' I took away a ring.'
Him Hagen questioned : ' Dost thou keep it
      still ? '
Siegfried replied : ' A lady weareth it.'
' Brunhilde ! ' muttered Hagen to himself.
Now Gunther spake : ' Naught, Siegfried, will I
      take
From thee as present ; all my goods were naught
To offer in exchange for what is thine.

Thy servant will I be without reward.'
And while they talked Gudrun came through
    the hall
Bearing a brimming goblet; then she said:
'My lord, the house of Gibich welcomes thee!
Its daughter brings thee drink.'   Then Siegfried
    bowed
Towards her with grave courtesy, and took
The cup, and held it from him for a space,
The whiles he murmured: 'Though I may forget
All thou hast taught me, yet there is the love
Implanted by thee, unforgettable!
Brunhilde, to our love I drink, and thee!'
He drained the cup, and gave it to Gudrun,
Whose downcast eyes refused to meet his gaze.
Then said Siegfried, with passion in his eyes,
'Thou whose bright glance hath stirred mine
    inmost heart,
Why dost thou cast thine eyes upon the ground?'
Thereat the blood rushed mantling to her face,
And Gudrun looked at Siegfried stedfastly.
Then cried the hero: 'Loveliest of girls,
Look down again!   The beauty of thine eyes
Hath set my heart aflame; I feel the blood
Rage madly through my veins!   Lord Gunther,
    say,

What is thy sister's name?'   And Gunther said:
'Gudrun.'   Then Siegfried cried aloud, and said:
'Are they good runes I read in her bright eyes?
Gudrun, I sware to be thy brother's man;
But he refused me proudly; wouldst thou, too,
Refuse me if I swore to live for thee?'
Then spake Gudrun no word, but drooped her
    head,
And slowly passed without the echoing hall.
And Siegfried watched her, spell-bound, while
    the twain,
Gunther and Hagen, kept watch on Siegfried.
Siegfried asked suddenly: 'Lord Gunther, pray,
Hast thou a wife?'   And Gunther answered
    him:
'No woman have I wooed; I have no hope
Of love and marriage, for my heart is set
On one whom no device can win for me.'
Then Siegfried quickly turned to him, and said:
'What should prevent thee if I stood thy friend?'
And Gunther said: 'Her home is on the fell,
And glowing fires surround her lonely home.'
Then Siegfried murmured, e'en as though the
    words
Were old, yet strange: 'Her home is on the fell,
And glowing fires surround her lonely home. . . .?'

And Gunther went on : 'Only he who braves
The fierceness of the flames . . .' Siegfried
   brake in :
''Tis only he who braves the hungry flames . . .'
'Can woo and win Brunhilde,' Gunther said :
'I cannot climb the fell ; I dare not face
The raging fires !' Then Siegfried started up,
Crying : 'I fear no fires, for thee I'll win
Thy dainty bride ; for am I not thy man ?
And all my strength is thine, if in return
Thou wilt bestow Gudrun upon thy friend.'
And Gunther said : 'Yea, gladly will I give
Gudrun to thee.' 'Brunhilde will I fetch,'
Said Siegfried. 'How wilt thou deceive the
   maid ?'
Asked Gunther. And the hero answered him :
'I will put on the Tarnhelm, and my form
Will then be thine.' 'Swear me an oath
   thereon !'
Cried Gunther. Siegfried said : 'Blood-brother-
   hood
I swear on oath to thee.' Then Hagen took
A horn and filled it nearly full with wine,
And Gunther and Siegfried laid bare their arms
And drew their swords. Then each one pricked
   his arm

And held it near the other's o'er the horn,
The whiles their blood dripped slowly in the
    wine.
Then sang the twain together: 'Glowing life's
Red blood is dripping down into the wine:
Hot with the burning fire of brotherhood
The red wine glows with blood! I pledge my
    troth
To thee, my friend; may brotherhood of blood
Be born to-day between us! If the bond
Be broken, let the red drops of our draught
Stream from the heart of him who spurns the
    troth!
And so I claim the compact, so I pledge
Unswerving faith to thee!' Thereat they drank,
Each half the wine and blood, and sealed the
    oath.
Then Hagen came up swiftly with his sword
And cleft the horn, whiles Gunther and Sieg-
    fried
Grasped each the other's hand. Then asked
    Siegfried
Of Hagen: 'Why wast thou not of the league?'
And Hagen said: 'Because my blood would
    taint
The sweetness of your drink; 'tis churlish blood,

So dull and heavy that my very cheek
It hardly reddens : baser men. must leave
High leagues to such as ye.'   Then Gunther
    said :
' Heed not the knave.'   And Siegfried cried
    aloud :
' Away, away !   The boat rides near the shore ;
Swiftly we 'll glide towards th'enchanted fell !
One night shalt thou await me ; then thy bride
Together we will bring to Gibich's halls.'
Then Gunther asked him : ' Wilt thou take no
    rest ? '
And Siegfried said : ' 'Twill rest me to return ;
Therefore I tarry not.'   He spake, and strode
With eager steps towards the river bank.
Then Gunther said to Hagen : ' In thine hands
I leave the house,' and straightway down the
    path
He followed after Siegfried.   Now Gudrun
Came from her room, and, seeing Hagen, said :
' Tell me, I pray thee, whither are they gone
So suddenly and swiftly ? '   Hagen said :
' To set Brunhilde free.'   Then sighed Gudrun :
' Is Siegfried gone ? '   And Hagen answered her :
' See how his love for thee doth urge him on
To win thee for his wife ! '   And then he took

His spear and shield, and sate down in the hall,
And watched the boat speed onwards through
    the gloom.
Then Gudrun softly said : ' Siegfried, mine own !'
And passed within the hangings to her place.
At last spake Hagen : ' Here I sit and watch
And guard the house, and ward foes from the
    land,
While Gibich's son is wafted by the winds
Upon his wooing bent.   A hero bold
Doth steer him, who will keep him from all
    harm ;
The hero brings his bride to father Rhine,
And gives her to his friend : he brings the ring
For me.   Ye gallant men, ye comrades true,
Sail merrily upon your journeyings !
He whom ye hold so cheap—the Nibelung—
His minions are ye both.'

.   .   .   .   .   .

                      Now near the cave
Upon the highland fell sate Brunhilde
Gazing in deepest thought upon the ring
Which Siegfried gave her as the plight of troth.
And ever and anon, o'ercome by love's
Sweet memories of passion-hours gone by,
She covered it with kisses.   Suddenly

She heard a distant sound, and turned her head
To listen whence it came. 'How well I know
That sound!' she cried; 'a horse is galloping
Towards me through the air; the thundering
     clouds
Strike echoes from the fell. I wonder who
Hath found my lonely home?' Then out of
     space
Valtraute's voice was borne upon the breeze:
'Sister! Brunhild'! Art sleeping or awake?'
Then sprang Brunhilde to her feet, and cried:
'Valtraute's voice! So well known and beloved:
Dear, daring girl, how brave of thee to come!
Go down into the wood below the rocks
And climb the hill when thou hast tied thine
     horse.
Dar'st thou come nigh me? Thou art very bold!
May thy poor sister kiss thee fearlessly?'
So spake Brunhilde as she ran to greet
Her sister; and the gladness in her eyes
Saw nothing of the other's misery.
Then said Valtraute: 'Hither I have sped
On thine account.' Brunhilde joyously
Spoke on: 'Was it alone for love of me
That thou hast dared to slight lord Wotan's ban,
Or why? O tell me! Hath my father's mood

Softened towards me? When despite the god
I shielded Siegmund, wrongfully, perchance,
I carried out my father's secret wish.
And that his wrath is passed I know full well;
For, though he bound mine eyes in sleep, and
    chained
My body to this rock, to be the prize
Of him who found and woke me, yet he heard
The voice of my entreaty, and with fire
He ringed the fell, so that faint-hearted men
Dared not come nigh me. Thus my punishment
Was turned to highest happiness, for he
Who found and won me is of all mankind
The noblest hero; through his love my life
Is filled with smiles and sunshine. Hath my fate
Enticed thee hither, sister? Dost thou pine
For love-bright days like mine? Wouldst thou,
    too, share
The pure content of loving hearts at peace?'
Valtraute answered: 'Share the foolishness
That holds thee fast? Nay, 'twas a weightier
    thing
Which drave me on to break great Wotan's law.'
Then said Brunhilde: 'Dread anxiety
Seemeth to crush thee, dear one? Is his wrath
Not yet abated? Doth his anger reach

From me to thee?'   Valtraute made reply:
'If 'twere but fear of him, anxiety
Had met a speedy end.'   Brunhilde said:
'I do not understand.'   The Valkyrie
Went on: 'Be not distressed, but hearken well
To what I have to say.   The anxious dread
Which drave me from Valhalla hitherwards
Urgeth me to return.'   Brunhilde cried:
'What fate hath come upon the deathless gods?'
Valtraute answered: 'Listen to my words.
Since thou and he were parted, never once
Hath Wotan's order sent us to the fight:
Downcast we rode unbidden to the host.
And Wotan shunned Valhalla's heroes brave,
And solitary roamed about the world
Ahorse, as Wanderer, and rested not.
Now is he just come home, and in his hand
He held the splinters of his ashen spear,
By mortal hands struck down.   With voiceless
     sign
He waved Valhalla's noblest to the grove
To make the world-ash die; he bade them pile
Its timbers in great stacks around our walls.
He called the gods to council; his high seat
He took, and called the tremblers to his side;
The thronging press of heroes filled the hall—

There sate he dumb, and spake no word to us,
With the spear's splinters clenched within his
    grasp;
He would not eat the apples Hilda brought;
The cold of fear and sorrow froze the gods.
His ravens twain he loosed upon the world,
And when they flew back with good news from
    far
A last smile lightened on the god's wan face.
We Valkyries lay clinging to his knees,
But he was blind to our imploring eyes,
And endless grief and terror seized our hearts.
Reckless I threw me weeping on his breast;
His fixed eye changed; his mind went back to
    thee!
Deeply he sighed, and closed his eyes, and spake
As though he dreamed: " If she would give the
    ring
Back to the daughters of deep-flowing Rhine
Both gods and world were lightened of the
    curse !"
I pondered on these words; then from his side
I stole away through ranks of silent gods;
Leaped on my horse and sped away to thee.
Sister, I do implore thee, put an end
To this great sorrow of the deathless ones!

Thou hast the power; the gods hang on thy will.'
Brunhilde answered: 'Thou poor, sad-faced child,
What wild dream-tales dost thou recount to me?
I am an exile from the cloudy heights
Where dwell our holy gods: I understand
No shred of thy lament.   By woe distraught
Thy mind is quivering; thy weary eyes
Are lit with sudden flashes of red fire.
My poor, pale sister with the wild wan face,
What wouldst thou have me do?'   Valtraute
    cried:
'That ring upon thine hand—that cursed ring!
Cast it away, for Wotan's sake, away!'
Brunhilde answered: 'Cast my ring away?'
'Yea,' cried Valtraute; 'give it back again
To the three daughters of deep-flowing Rhine!'
Then said Brunhilde: 'Thou wouldst have me
    give
To alien folk the love-pledge Siegfried gave?
Thou must be mad to crave such boons of me.'
Valtraute answered: 'Listen to my grief;
The world's unrest is stirred up by thy ring!
Hurl it then from thee far into the flood,
And end Valhalla's misery!   Hurl forth
The cursèd thing far out into the flood!'
Then cried Brunhilde: 'Canst thou understand

What my ring is to me? How couldst thou
    know,
Thou poor, cold maid! My ring is more to me
Than all Valhalla's bliss, than all the fame
Pertaining to the gods; one fleeting glance
At its bright sheen, one gleam from its pure
    gold
Are more to me than the eternal peace
Of all the deathless gods! For Siegfried's love
Shines out therefrom upon me — Siegfried's
    love!
'Tis only love can tell thee of its strength!
The ring abides with me. Go back again
And face the mighty council of the gods.
Thus tell them of my ring: my love and I
Are one for ever; when they take from me
My love Valhalla crumbles to the dust!'
Then asked Valtraute: 'Dost thou mean these
    words?
Wilt leave thy sister loveless in her woe?'
Brunhilde answered: 'Speed thee home again;
Get to thine horse; thou wilt not have my ring.'
Then cried Valtraute: ''Tis a tale of woe!
Woe to thee, sister, woe to all the gods.'
She spake, and fled away, and from the wood
Brunhilde heard the gallop of her steed.

Now storm clouds, red with thunder, crossed the
     sky,
And passed in dread array towards the west.
Brunhilde, watching, cried : ' Ye wind-blown
     clouds,
Compact of fire and thunder, pass away !
Steer not your course to me !'   So fell the dusk,
And Wotan's fires gleamed redder in the gloom.
' Twilight's dark shadows shroud the heavens'
     face ;
The guardian flames seem climbing up the fell :
Why creeps the glowing circle o'er its bounds ?
The fearsome fires come surging on and on !'
Now from the vale a horn's note sounded clear.
Then leaped Brunhilde to her feet, and cried :
' Siegfried ! dear Siegfried is come back to me !
I know his call !   Away, and lie again
Within his godlike arms !' she dashed away
To meet her lover, while the red-tongued flames
Licked higher and still higher.   Suddenly
From out their midst sprang Siegfried, and the
     fires
Sank slowly down to their accustomed place.
Now Siegfried wore the Tarnhelm, and his form
Was that of Gunther.   Then Brunhilde cried :
' I am betrayed !   Who hath invaded me ?'

And backwards ran, then gazed with speechless
    fear
On Siegfried.   And her husband, for a space,
Leaned on his spear and looked at her, then spake
In feigned deep tones: 'Brunhilde! there is
    come
A suitor to thee, whom no fire of thine
Can frighten back.   Thee for my wife I woo;
Accept me willingly!'   Brunhilde asked:
'Who art thou who hast done what only one
Was given power to do?'   Siegfried replied:
'A hero, who will tame thy mood by force,
If only force can tame thee.'   Then his wife
Was struck with terror: 'On yon stone there
    stands
A demon!   'Tis an eagle in man's guise
Flown up to rend my flesh!   What art thou, say!
Art thou a man, or art thou of the host
From Hella's night-dark shades?'   Siegfried re-
    plied:
'I am a Gibichung, and he whom thou
Must follow is called Gunther.'   Then Brunhild',
Tortured by wild despair, brake into sobs:
'Wotan, most harsh of fathers and of gods!
Alas! the meaning of thy doom is plain!
To shame and sorrow hast thou cast me forth!'

Then came Siegfried towards her, whiles he
    said :
'The night draws on, and thou must wed with
    me.'
Then menacingly did his wife stretch forth
Her finger, whereon glittered Siegfried's ring,
And cried : 'Approach not !   Be thou 'ware this
    pledge !
To shame thou canst not bring me, while the
    ring
My guardian is.'   Then Siegfried laughed in
    scorn :
''Twill serve to give to Gunther husband's
    rights :
Yea, with the ring to him shalt thou be wed !'
Then cried Brunhilde : 'Robber, touch me not !
Come not thou near me ; steel is not so strong
As I when guarded by the ring, and it
Thou ne'er shalt take away !'   Then said Sieg-
    fried :
'Thou teachest me to take away thy ring.'
He spoke, and rushed upon her, and the twain
Grappled like wrestlers, till at length Brunhild'
Brake loose and fled.   But Siegfried caught her
    up
And held her with one arm, the whiles he tore

The ring from off her hand.   Then shrieked
    Brunhild'
And fell exhausted on the stony ground.
But Siegfried cried in triumph : ' Thou art mine !
' Brunhilde, Gunther's bride, now shalt thou
    share
With me thy lonely bed ! '   Brunhilde moaned :
' Thou wretched woman, where is help for thee ? '
Trembling she did the bidding of her lord,
And went within the cave.   Then Siegfried drew
His sword, and cried in his own voice aloud :
' Needful, be witness of my purity !
Keep thou the oath I sware unto my friend,
And set thyself between me and his bride ! '
So saying, Siegfried went within the cave.

ACT II

BEFORE the palace of the Gibichungs
Sate Hagen, sleeping, and the moon's soft glow
Lit up the puny form of Alberich,
Crouched down beside his knees.   Then said the
    dwarf:
'Hagen, my son, art sleeping?   Dost thou sleep
And hearkenest not to me, whom sleep and
    sloth
Have ruined?'   Hagen spake as though he
    slept:
'I hear thee, thou sad gnome, what hast to say
That may inform my dreams?'   Said Alberich:
'I would remind thee of the wondrous strength
Thou hast at thy command, inherited
From her who was thy mother and my wife.'
Him Hagen answered: 'Though my mother gave
This boasted strength, I will not give her thanks,
In that she listened to thine amorous wiles.
Bloodless, untimely old, and wizened up,
I hate the joyous, knowing naught of joy!'

Then said his sire : 'Yea, Hagen, thou art right
To hate the happy, for thus shalt thou love
As thou shouldst love thy father, robed in grief,
Outworn with sorrow.   Be thou bold and false ;
They against whom we wage war secretly
Shall feel ere long the keen stab of our hate.
That prince of robbers, Wotan, who did steal
Thy ring from me, was lately put to flight
By one of his own brood : the Volsung took
His pomp and glory from him ; he is 'ware
That he and all his sort are surely doomed.
I fear him not ; he 'll fall with all the rest !
Hagen, my son, art sleeping ?'   Hagen asked :
'Who is the heir to the eternal power ?'
'Myself, and thou !' cried Alberich ; 'the world
Lies at our feet, if only I am sure
Of thy good faith in sharing weal and woe.'
'Twas this same Volsung brake great Wotan's
     spear—
He who the dragon, Fafner, did to death
And took the ring to play with, as a child
Takes any pretty toy.   Now is he lord
Of everything ; Valhalla and the dwarfs
Alike bow down before him, and my curse
Falls harmless on this fearless hero's head.
For he knows nothing of the ring's true worth,

And makes no use of its tremendous power;
He thinks of naught but love and such like stuff:
To ruin him must be our first concern.
Hagen, my son, dost hear me?' Hagen said:
'Already have I helped him to his doom.'
'Ah! that gold ring! 'tis that we must obtain!'
Cried Alberich: 'but Siegfried is beloved
By a wise woman; if she counsel him
To give the Rhine's fair daughters back their
　　　ring—
The same who fooled me in the waters' depths—
The ring is lost; no cunning can avail.
Therefore, delay not, make the ring thine aim.
I bred thee fearless that in times of stress
Against great heroes thou mightst be my stay.
Doubtless thou wast not strong enough to slay
The dragon; only Siegfried could do that,
Yet deathless hate is stronger than men's
　　　strength,
And that I bred in thee; thou shalt avenge
Thy father, and win back the magic ring,
And put to scorn the Volsung and Wotan!
Hagen, my son, wilt swear an oath thereto?'
Him Hagen answered: 'Set thy mind at rest;
I'll get the ring!' But Alberich replied:
'Swear it, then, Hagen, swear it, then, my son!'

So Hagen said: 'I swear it by myself;
Now art thou satisfied?'   And Alberich said,
As in the morning mists he disappeared:
'Hagen, my son, be true!   My trusty lad,
Be true!   Be true!'   The sun rose over Rhine,
And Hagen still sate staring into space.
Now presently from out the river bed
Came Siegfried, with the Tarnhelm in his belt,
Crying, 'Ho! Hagen! thou most sleepy loon!
Dost see who 'tis?'   Then Hagen rose and said:
'Well, Siegfried! speedy hero, whence art thou?'
'From Brunhild's fell,' cried Siegfried; 'there I
    drew
The breath with which I woke thee, for I came
Like lightning!   Slower come the other twain
Aboard their boat.'   'Hast captured fair Brun-
    hild'?'
Asked Hagen.   Siegfried said: 'Where is
    Gudrun?'
Then Hagen shouted: 'Ho! Gudrun! Gudrun!
Come out, Siegfried is here; why stay within?'
Then Siegfried turned towards the house and said:
'I'll tell ye twain how I obtained Brunhild'.'
For Gudrun came to meet him, and he said:
'Wilt thou not bid me welcome, Gibich maid?
I have good news for thee.'   Then said Gudrun:

' Freia, the women's goddess, give thee joy ! '
And Siegfried said : ' Be happy in my joy ;
For this day have I won thee for my wife.'
But Gudrun made as though she heard him not,
And asked : ' Doth Gunther hither bring Brun-
     hild' ? '
And Siegfried answered : ' Ay, his bride was won
Right easily.'   And Gudrun asked again :
' Did not the fire burn him ? '   Siegfried said :
' 'Twould not have harmed him, but for him I
     crossed
The fiery belt, because I wanted thee.'
Then asked Gudrun : ' And didst thou pass un-
     harmed ? '
' I loved the waving brightness,' said Siegfried.
Gudrun made question : ' Did Brunhild' believe
That thou wert Gunther ? '   Siegfried answered
     her :
' I matched him to a hair ; the feat was done
Through the Tarnhelm, as Hagen prophesied.'
And Hagen said : ' Therein I counselled well.'
Then Gudrun asked : ' Did this fierce girl
     submit
Without a struggle ? '   Siegfried answered her :
' She bowed to Gunther's strength.'   Then said
     Gudrun :

‘ And did she lie with thee ? ’   Siegfried replied :
‘ Through the long bridal night Brunhild’
    obeyed
Her husband.’   Gudrun cried : ‘ But she believed
That thou wert he ! ’   He answered her :
    ‘ Siegfried
Was waiting for Gudrun.’   ‘ And yet,’ said she,
‘ Brunhild’ was by his side ? ’   Then said Siegfried :
‘ ’Twixt east and west there lies the distant
    north ;
So near or far was Brunhilde from him.’
‘ And how did Gunther take his bride from thee ? ’
‘ At peep of day across the burning zone
Towards the misty vale she followed me :
Anigh the river Gunther changed his form
To mine, and I to his ; no eye could mark
The change, so swift it was.   Then at my wish
The magic helmet brought me back to thee.
A strong wind drives the lovers up the stream ;
Prepare to welcome them ! ’   Then said Gudrun :
‘ Siegfried, most mighty of all living men,
What fear I feel for thee ! ’   And Hagen cried :
‘ Far in the distance I can see a sail ! ’
‘ Then thank the zealous herald ! ’ laughed
    Siegfried.
But Gudrun said : ‘ Her welcome shall be warm,

That she may dwell contented in our midst.
Hagen, go summon all the country-side
To the big hall to make the marriage-feast,
And I will bid the women; in our joy
They will show gladness.'   As she turned to go
Towards the hall she passed Siegfried, and said:
'Thou wicked hero, wilt thou take no rest?'
And Siegfried said: 'To help thee is to rest.'
And followed her within the echoing hall.

        .   .   .   .   .   .

Then Hagen went upon a height and turned
Towards the hills, and blew his cattle-horn;
'Hoiho! hoiho! hoiho! ye Gibich men
Come hither quickly!   Danger stalks abroad!
The foe is up!   Quick, arm ye! arm ye, quick!
Bring goodly weapons, sharp for instant war,
For time is pressing, danger's in the air!
'Hoiho! hoiho! hoiho!'   He blew again
A   long-drawn   blast.   From   every   rift   there
        came
Horns answering; from valley and from hill
Armed men ran hurriedly.   The vassals cried:
'Why   sounds   the   horn?   who   calls   us   to   the
        host?
We   come   with   weapons   sharp   and   strong   and
        true!

Hoiho! hoiho! Hagen! what foe is near?
What danger presseth?   Who is come to fight?
Doth Gunther stand in need?'   Then Hagen
    cried:
'Arm ye, and tarry not; a welcome sure
Shall Gunther give ye; he hath won a wife.'
'Is he hard pressed by foes?' the vassals cried.
And Hagen answered: 'He hath brought him
    home
A wayward wife.'   The vassals cried again:
'Doth the red maw of foemen trouble him?'
And Hagen answered: 'He doth come alone;
No enemy pursueth.'   Then they cried:
'Hath he lost all things on a stricken field?'
And Hagen said: 'The slayer of the beast—
Siegfried, the hero—kept him safe from harm.'
Then said the vassals: 'Can the host avail
To holpen him?'   And Hagen answered them:
'Great bullocks shall ye slay, and drench with
    blood
Lord Wotan's altar.'   Then the vassals asked:
'Hagen, why didst thou call us?'   Hagen said:
'To kill a boar for Froh, and eke a goat
For Donner; for my lady Fricka sheep
Shall ye prepare, that she may bless the bride!'
Thereat the peasants laughed, and asked again:

'When we have slain the beasts what shall we
    do?'
And Hagen answered : 'Take the loving-cup,
Brimful of mead and wine, from ladies' hands.'
The vassals questioned : 'When we hold the cup
What wouldst thou have us do?' Then Hagen
    said :
'Drink yourselves drunk as quickly as ye may ;
All for the honour of th' immortal gods,
That they may bless the marriage !' Then the
    swains
Laughed long and loud, and cried : 'Good luck
    is come
For certain to the Rhine when Hagen grim
Thinks fit to crack his joke ! The Hardy Thorn
Hath given up his pricking, and is set
On marriage-feasts, forsooth !' Yet no smile
    dawned
On Hagen's face, as to the men he said :
'Stop laughing, my brave lads, and go to meet
Your liege-lord's bride ; Brunhilde cometh nigh.
Love ye your lady, and be true to her ;
If ever she receive an injury
Let your revenge be swift and terrible !'

    .   .   .   .   .   .

Now Gunther and Brunhilde neared the shore ;

And bare-legged yeomen dragged the boat to
    land,
Amid a din of shouts and clashing arms—
'Hail, welcome, hail!' a thousand voices cried:
'Hail to thee, Gunther, hail to thy fair bride!'
Then Gunther led Brunhilde from the boat,
And said: 'I bring to you and to the Rhine
Brunhilde, fairest daughter of her race;
A nobler wife was never won by man.
The gods have looked with favour on our house,
And blessed the sons of Gibich, but our fame
Is now assured for ever!'   Then a shout
Rose up to heaven from the vassal-crowd:
'Hail, Gunther, hail!   Most lucky Gibichung!'
Then passed Brunhilde, pale, with downcast eyes,
With Gunther towards the palace, and a train
Of ladies issued from the moated keep
Behind Gudrun and Siegfried.   'Hail! my lord!'
Cried Gunther; 'Hail, Gudrun!   How glad am I
To see thee by his side who hath obtained
Thine hand in marriage!   Here are four hearts
    twain—
Brunhild' and Gunther, Gudrun and Siegfried!'
Thereat Brunhilde started, as men start
When certain death confronts them suddenly,
And looking up she saw 'twas Siegfried there.

Then dropped she Gunther's hand, and took a
    step
Towards him, fury blazing in her eyes ;
Then backwards went again with eyes dull-set
In speechless, stony horror.   And the crowd
Cried : ' Look ye ! she is ailing !'   And Siegfried
Advanced towards her, saying : 'What doth cloud
Brunhilde's brow ?'   Scarce mistress of herself
Brunhilde cried : ' Siegfried ? what means . . .
    Gudrun . . . ?'
And Siegfried said : ' She is the Gibich maid,
Betrothed to me, as Gunther is to thee.'
Then cried Brunhilde : ' I ? . . . Betrothed ? . . .
    Siegfried,
Thou liest !   O ! 'tis growing dark ! . . .'   She
    fell,
But Siegfried caught and held her in his arms.
There faintly murmured she : ' Now let me die,
For Siegfried doth not know me !'   And Siegfried
Called Gunther, saying : ' Look thou to thy wife,
For she is fainting.'   To Brunhild' he said :
' Lady, awake ! thy husband is with thee.'
Now as he pointed with his outstretched hand
To Gunther Brunhild' saw the magic ring
Gleaming upon his finger, and she cried
With voice that frightened all the listening folk :

'Ha! 'tis the ring! . . . On *his* hand! . . . Sieg-
    fried's hand!'
And all the peasants, crowding eagerly,
Asked each the other: 'What is i' the wind?'
Then Hagen strode up from behind the mob
And loudly shouted: 'Give ear, all of ye,
To what the dame shall say!'   Then did Brun-
    hild',
Stifling the storm of passion in her breast,
Look fixedly at Siegfried, and spake thus:
'Upon thine hand I saw a ring; that ring
Is not thine own; by force 'twas reft from me
By him thou callest Gunther.   Canst thou say
How thou didst get the ring?'   Then said Sieg-
    fried:
'From Gunther I did not obtain the ring.'
Then cried Brunhild' to Gunther: 'Didst not
    thou
Wrest that same ring from me, and by its power
Force me to do thy will?   If so, regain
The ring which thou hast won, and keep thine
    own!'
Thereat was Gunther puzzled, and he said:
'The ring?   I gave him none: how dost thou
    know
This stranger-guest?'   Brunhilde answered him:

I

'Where hast thou hid the ring didst win from
    me?'
And Gunther spake no word.   Then cried Brun-
    hild':
'Ha! then 'twas he who robbed me of my ring!
'Twas Siegfried, treacherous thief!'   And Sieg-
    fried said:
'No woman gave the golden ring to me;
I did not take the ring from woman's hand;
It was the meed of battle, won in fight
From the fierce dragon of the Cave of Hate.'
Then Hagen came between them, and he said:
'Lady Brunhilde, thou must know right well
This ring of thine?   If this should be the ring
Thou gav'st to Gunther, then 'tis Gunther's own,
And Siegfried hath obtained it by a trick
For which the traitor shall receive reward!'
Then shrieked Brunhilde in her agony:
'A trick!   Ay! shamefullest of wicked tricks!
Deceit beyond imagining!   Betrayed,
I yet will be revenged!'   Then asked Gudrun:
'Who hath deceived thee?'   And the wonder-
    ing crowd
Cried: 'Who is thy betrayer?'   Then Brunhild'
Answered them thus: 'Ye gods that rule the
    sky,

Lords of high heaven, did your whispered will
Intend this suffering? Ye have taught me grief
Such as none other felt; profounder depths
Of shame ne'er overwhelmed a woman's soul;
Grant me, I pray, a fulness of revenge
Unknown until this hour! Light up in me
A flame of searing wrath unquenchable!
Tear out my heart, if ruin only thus
May come on him who hath betrayed my love!'
Then Gunther sought to soothe her furious mood,
Saying: 'Brunhilde, dear one, calm thyself!'
But she disdained him, crying: 'Traitor, hence!
Thou art thyself betrayed! Know all of ye
That not your lord, but he who standeth there
Is wed to me.' Thereat the country-folk
Cried: 'Siegfried? He is wedded to Gudrun!'
She answered: 'He hath wrought his lustful
    will
On me!' Then brake in Siegfried: 'Since thy-
    self
Art heedless of thy fame, I must thrust back
Upon thy lips the lie that threatens it.
Listen, and judge if I have broken faith!
With Gunther did I swear blood-brotherhood,
And Needful, my good sword, maintained the
    oath,

Set keen-edged 'twixt me and this sad-faced
    dame.'
Then cried Brunhilde : ' Hero of deceits,
What paltry lie is this ?   In vain thy sword
Thou callest to thine aid !   I know the blade ;
I know the scabbard too, wherein it hung
Upon the wall what time its guileful lord
Was winning love from her he hath betrayed ! '
Then anger stirred the hearts of all the throng :
' How now ?   Hath this man broken faith with
    us ?
Hath Gunther's honour suffered at his hands ? '
And Gunther, stern-faced, said: ' I am disgraced,
The butt of mocking foes, if in thy mouth
There is not wherewithal to answer her.'
And Gudrun cried : ' O Siegfried, say 'tis false !
Thou couldst not be unfaithful ! '   And the
    throng
Murmured with many voices : ' Right thyself,
If thou art in the right ; upon thine oath
Deny the charge.'   Then Siegfried answered
    them :
' Upon mine oath I do deny the charge :
Which among you will lend a sword or spear
That I may swear thereon ? '   And Hagen
    said :

' Here is my spear; swear thou upon its point;
'Twill guard the oath in honour.'   Then the
    men
Made a clear space, and Hagen held the spear
Towards Siegfried, and the hero touched the
    point
With his right hand, and said : ' Bright weapon
    pure,
Help me to swear an oath forever true !
By this unsullied spear-point do I swear,
And do thou listen, spear-point, to my words :
Where steel can strike, do thou strike home in
    me,
Where death can find me, do thou deal me death
If what this woman saith be good and true
And I have rent the bonds of brotherhood !'
Then rushed Brunhilde through the thronging
    press
And brake into the ring, and tore the hand
Of Siegfried from the spear, and set her own
Upon the point, and cried : ' Bright weapon pure,
Help me to swear an oath forever true !
By this unsullied spear-point do I swear,
And do thou listen, spear-point, to my words :
Thy strength to Siegfried's death I consecrate ;
Blest is the sharpness that shall let his blood ;

For he hath broken every sacred bond,
And sworn a false oath by thy sacred self!'
Then were the people greatly set in awe,
Crying: 'Help, Donner, make thy thunderings,
And drown the voice of shame!'   But Siegfried
    said:
'Gunther, I pray thee take care of thy wife,
Who falsely would impute this infamy.
Let the wild mountain-girl have rest and peace,
That this her fury may forget itself,
Which demon's spite hath raised against us all!
Go home, my men, and leave this woman's talk!
We soon shall be a set of poor poltroons
If we go fighting often tongue-wise thus!'
Then coming close to Gunther's side, he said:
'Troth! it hath hurt me even more than thee
That I disguised myself so carelessly:
Now certain am I that the Tarnhelm hid
But half of me.   Yet woman's anger dies
With morrow's light; soon will she give me
    thanks
That I have won her for thee.'   To the folk
He turned again, and cried: 'Make merry, men!
Follow me to the feast!   Ye women, help
To swell the marriage-triumph!   Sunny days
Smile down upon us; I will foremost be

To frolic in the palace and the grove!
Let him whom love hath blessed look on my
    joy,
And in remembrance of his own be glad.'
He spake, and put his arm around Gudrun,
And drew her lovingly towards the hall.
And after them the host of vassals came.
But Gunther and Brunhilde stayed behind
With Hagen, and great sorrow fell on them.
There mused Brunhilde: 'What demoniac spite
Is hidden in these things?   What magic spell
Raised up this storm?   Where is the power of
    mind
To combat this bewitchment?   Where the wit
To solve this riddle?   O 'tis misery!
Woe's me!   My wisdom gave I all to him;
He hath me in his power; within his toils
My heart is snared, yet am I tossed aside
And given to another!   Where's a sword,
That I may cut my bonds?'   Then Hagen came
Close up to her, and said: Have trust in me,
Thou lady wronged!   For thou shalt be re-
    venged.'
'On whom?' Brunhilde asked him.   Hagen said:
'On Siegfried, who betrayed thee.'   Then she
    laughed,

A hard and bitter laugh : ' Dost think that
    thou
Couldst vengeance wreak on Siegfried ?   One
    fierce glance
From those bright eyes of his—that 'spite the
    helm
Gleamed down on me—would cow thy finest
    pluck ! '
Hagen made answer : ' He hath falsely sworn
' Upon my spear, and it will be avenged ! '
Brunhilde cried : ' What idle words are these—
" Oath," and " false oath " !   Look thou for
    stronger means
Wherewith to point the temper of thy spear
If thou wouldst vanquish Siegfried ! ' Hagen said :
' Full well I know the might that is Siegfried's,
And that to slay him fighting face to face
Were nigh impossible ; yet whisper me
Some secret counsel whereby strength may fall
To cunning.'   Then Brunhilde cried aloud :
' O thankless love !   Untold ingratitude !
There was no art that I was mistress of
I did not make the guardian of his life !
No thought of future vengeance chilled my heart ;
My magic made him safe from every wound.'
Then Hagen asked : ' Can nothing injure him ? '

Brunhilde answered : 'Nothing can avail
To harm him save a blow struck from behind !
I knew that he would never flinch aside,
Nor, fleeing, turn his back towards his foe ;
Wherefore I laid no spell upon him there.'
'And there my spear shall reach him !' Hagen
    cried,
And turned to Gunther, saying : 'Come away,
Most noble Gibichung ! Thy lady wife
Awaits thee ; why dost hang thy head in grief?'
Then Gunther rose up heavily, and said :
'Shame ! shame and sorrow ! Naught but woe
    is mine,
The wretchedest of men !' And Hagen said :
'Alas ! 'tis true that thou art come to shame !'
Brunhilde cried : 'Thou coward and false friend !
Behind the hero didst thou hide thyself
To win the meed of valour ! Low is sunk
Thy once proud race, since thou art of its stock !'
Then waxed lord Gunther furious, and cried :
'Betrayer am I—and I am betrayed !
Deceiver am I—and I am deceived !
My marrow melts within me, and my heart
Is torn in twain ! Help, Hagen ! Find a way
To save mine honour ! Help thy mother's son !'
Him Hagen answered : 'No brain can avail

To help thee, nay, nor hand : one thing alone
Can profit thee, and that is Siegfried's death !'
Then   Gunther   cried   astonied: 'Siegfried's
    death ?'
And Hagen said : 'His death can expiate
Thy shame, but only death.'   Then Gunther
    stared
Before him horror-struck ; at last he said :
'We   swore   blood-brotherhood.'   And Hagen
    cried :
'Blood must avenge the breaking of the oath !'
Then Gunther asked : 'When did he break the
    oath ?'
And   Hagen   answered : 'When thou wert
    betrayed.'
'Did he betray me ?' asked the Gibichung.
'He did betray thee,' answered him Brunhild' :
'And I by all of ye have been betrayed !
The blood of all the world could not atone
For your offence, yet one death shall suffice
For all ; Siegfried shall die, to expiate
His sins and yours !'   Then Hagen turned aside
To Gunther, saying : 'Thou wilt profit much
By Siegfried's fall ; tremendous power is thine
If thou but seize his ring, which only death
Will part from him.'   'It is Brunhilde's ring ?'

Asked Gunther.   Hagen said : ' The Nibelungs
Lay claim to it.'   Then Gunther sighed, and said :
' Shall this be Siegfried's ending ? '   Hagen
    snarled :
' His death will be a blessing to us all.'
' But poor Gudrun ! ' cried Gunther, ' whom I gave
To him in marriage ?   If we slay her spouse
How shall we stand before her ? '   Then Brunhild'
Cried in her rage : ' What are my runes to me ?
What boots me wisdom ?   Helpless in my grief
I see the truth ; the wizard is Gudrun,
And she hath taken Siegfried from my side !
May pain and sorrow be her lot for aye ! '
Then Hagen said to Gunther : ' Lest his death
Should grieve her, we will cover up the deed.
To-morrow will we go out for a hunt ;
Siegfried will wander from us, and a boar
Will kill him.'   Then did Gunther and Brunhild'
Cry both together : ' Yea, thus shall it be !
Siegfried shall die ; his blood shall wash away
The wrong that he hath done me !   Oath and
    faith
Hath he betrayed ; his punishment is death !
Thou god of vengeance !   Witness of men's oaths !
Come hither, Wotan !   Send thine awful host
To hearken to the oath of our revenge ! '

And Hagen muttered : 'Yea, so shall it be ;
Siegfried shall fall, and his brave heart shall die !
The hoard is mine ; it must belong to me,
And therefore from him must I wrest the ring !
Thou elfin father !   Mighty prince deposed !
Night watcher, lord of all the little men !
Heed what I say !   Bid all the Nibelungs
To pay thee due allegiance, for the ring
Is   once   more   thine ! '   Then   Gunther   and
    Brunhild'
Went to the palace slowly, silently ;
But Hagen stayed there, plotting sudden death.

ACT III

WHERE Rhine runs swiftly through the wooded
    hills
His daughters dallied idly with the flood;
And as they swam their mazy dance they sang:
'Dear Mother Sun, we pray thee, brightly shine,
For night lies heavy on our gloomy depths.
Once were they light, for then our father's gold
Lay sparkling there; Rhine gold! thou best of
    gold!
How bravely didst thou beam in olden days,
Thou clear star of the deeps! Dear Mother
    Sun,
Send us the hero who will give us back
Our long lost gold!   If it were ours again
We would not ask to see thy gleaming eye!
Rhine gold! bright gold!   Thou wouldst be
    shining then,
Thou clear star of the deeps!'
                              Woglinde cried:
'I hear the horn of Siegfried!'   'It is nigh,'

Answered Wellgunde. Then Flosshilde said:
'Let us take counsel.' So beneath the flood
They dived all three. And Siegfried reached
the cliff
And said: 'Some imp hath led me all astray,
For I have lost the tracks; I wonder where
The rogue hath hid my quarry?' Then the
nymphs
Rose through the waters, calling: 'Ho!
Siegfried!'
'Why dost thou scold the mountain?' cried
Flosshild'.
Wellgunde cried: 'What imp hath baffled thee?'
And then Woglinde teased him, calling out:
'Was it a gnome that did it?' And all three
Cried out: 'Do tell us, Siegfried!' Laughingly
The hero looked down at them, and he said:
'Doubtless ye charmed away my furry friend
Who hath so strangely vanished? If by chance
He be your lover, to his ladies fair
I leave him willingly!' Thereat the nymphs
Laughed much. At length Woglinde said to
him:
'Siegfried, what wilt thou give us in return
For thy lost quarry?' Siegfried answered her:
'I have no purse; yet say, what would ye have?'

Wellgunde said: 'Upon thy finger gleams
A golden ring.'   Then all together cried:
'Give us the ring!'   But Siegfried answered
      them:
'A dragon did I slay to get this ring:
Think ye the paws of some old mangy bear
Are worth the bartering?'   Woglinde asked:
'Art thou so mean?'   'And stingy in a deal?'
Wellgunde added.   Flosshilde went on:
'Women prefer the generous sort of men.'
Siegfried replied: 'My wife would scold me well
If I did give her precious ring to you.'
'Is she so very strict?' Flosshilde asked.
Wellgunde laughed: 'Doubtless she beateth
      thee!'
Woglinde, too, made merry: 'He hath felt
'Her heavy hand ere this!'   And so they
      laughed.
'Laugh away now,' said Siegfried; 'when I go
Perchance ye will be crying, for the ring
Will go with me.'   Whereat Flosshilde sighed:
'He is so fair!'   Wellgunde made her moan:
'He is so strong!'   Woglinde murmured low:
'I think that I could love him!'   Then the th
Shouting together: ''Tis a crying shame
That he is stingy!' dived beneath the strea

And eddying ripples closed upon their jibes.
Then Siegfried went still lower down the slope,
And said : ''Tis hard that they should think me
　　mean ;
I cannot bear it ; if they rise again
I 'll let them have the ring !   Ye jocund sprites
Come hither quickly !   Ye shall have the ring ! '
Then rose again the daughters of the Rhine
With faces stern and grave. 'Siegfried,' said
　　they,
' Keep thou the ring, and keep it carefully,
Till thou hast felt the fulness of the curse
That dwells within it.   On that fateful day
Thou wilt be sorry that we freed thee not.'
Then on his finger Siegfried put the ring,
Saying : ' Now tell me all ye have to say.'
Then sadly sang the daughters of the stream :
' O Siegfried, Siegfried ! sorrow dogs thee down !
To thine undoing thou dost keep the ring
Fashioned from gold that glowed in father
　　Rhine ;
For he who shaped it by his cunning art,
And lost it to his shame, hath laid a curse
On it for all time, to drag to death
Its owner for the nonce.   The dragon fell ;
So too wilt fall ; yea, thou wilt fall to-day

Unless to us thou givest up the ring
To hide in deepest Rhine; his stream alone
Can wash away the spell!'   Siegfried replied:
'Ye clever ladies, ye need say no more!
I did not trust your flattery; your threats
Weigh even less with me.'   The Rhine nymphs
  cried:
'O Siegfried, Siegfried, we have told thee true!
Turn from the ban!   'Twas woven by the Norns
By night upon the endless rope of fate.'
Siegfried made answer: 'I have got a sword
That hath destroyed a spear; if in this rope—
This endless rope of fate—are woven bans,
Needful shall cut it for the weaving Norns!
I mind me how the dragon spake to me
Anent the curse; yet was he powerless
To teach me fear!   I was to be the heir
Of all the world because I owned the ring;
And yet I'd gladly give it up again
For love and love's delights; it had been yours
If ye had talked of love.   But menaces
'Gainst life and limb ye hurl at me instead;
And though it were not worth a single rush,
Ye shall not have the ring!   For life and limbs—
If loveless, bound by fear's consuming chains—
Look ye!   So would I throw them far from me!'

And Siegfried stooped and took a clod of earth
And threw it far behind him.   Then the nymphs
Cried out: 'Come, sisters, let this dullard be!
He boasts himself as mighty and as wise
As he is blind and trammelled.   He hath sworn
Oaths, and he hath not kept them; he hath
    known
Runes, and he hath not heeded their intent.
Of the great destiny to him bequeathed
And by him scorned he still is ignorant;
Only this ring, that dogs him to his death,
This ring alone his heart is set to have!
Siegfried, farewell!   To-day a lady proud
Will be the heir of thee and all that's thine:
She will obey us better.   So away,
Away to her!'   And so they swam away,
Still singing.   Siegfried watched them with a
    smile:
'In water and on land I've learned the ways
Of women; him who scorneth flatteries
They seek to fright with threats; when both
    have failed
They cover him with venom.   Yet, I wis,
Were it not treason to my fair Gudrun,
I had not loitered in the capturing
Of one of those sweet maids!'   A hunting horn

Sounded across the valley from the hills;
And Siegfried answered with a lusty call.
First Hagen reached the summit of the ridge,
And cried: 'Hoiho!   At last we find the nest
Where thou hast flown!'   And Siegfried shouted
    back:
'Come down!   Here blow the breezes fresh and
    cool!'
Then Hagen came and said: 'Let's rest a while
And eat and drink our fill.   Put down the game
And broach the wine-flasks!'   So the men set
    down
The deer and boars, and passed the wine-skin
    round.
Said Hagen presently: ''Twas Siegfried scared
Our game away; methinks he must have got
Some wondrous prize.'   Then Siegfried laughed,
    and said:
'I shall fare hardly if my meal depends
Upon my bag; I crave a share of thine.'
'Hast nothing?'   queried Hagen.   Siegfried
    said:
'I went forth to the woods, yet water-fowl
Alone I saw; if I had stalked them well
I might have caught ye three wild water-birds
Who sang to me down there on father Rhine

That I should die this day.'   Whereat the face
Of Gunther sicklied o'er, as furtively
He glanced at Hagen, who made answer thus:
' Most luckless hunter he, who bootyless
Is slain by lurking beasts.'   Then said Siegfried:
' I thirst.'   Whereat the brothers handed him
Their drinking-horns, for they on either side
Of him were sitting.   Hagen presently
Asked Siegfried, saying: ' I have often heard
That thou canst understand the song of birds;
What truth is in the tale?'   Siegfried replied:
' 'Tis long since I have given heed to learn
The meaning of their prattle'; and reached
    forth   .
His drinking-horn to Gunther, as he said:
' Drink, Gunther, drink!   Thy brother gives it
    thee.'
Into the horn looked Gunther gloomily:
' The wine is weak and pale; thy blood alone
Is mixed therein!'   Then Siegfried laughed, and
    said:
' With thine I'll mix it!' and took Gunther's
    horn
And poured into his own, until the wine
Ran over.   Then cried Siegfried merrily:
' Now doth it overflow!   To Mother Earth

I give it for her comfort!'   Gunther sighed:
'Thou overjoyous heart!'   And Siegfried said
To Hagen: 'Hath Brunhilde troubled him?'
Hagen made answer: 'Her he understands
As well as thou the prattle of the birds!'
Said Siegfried: 'Since I heard fair women sing
I have not given heed unto the birds.'
Hagen went on: 'Yet once upon a time
Thou understood'st their sayings?'   Siegfried
      cried:
'What ho! there, Gunther, gloomiest of men!
Will it amuse thee if I tell the tale
Of my young days?'   And Gunther answered
      him:
'I'd hear thee gladly.'   So they all sate round
While Siegfried told the story of his youth.
'A surly dwarf called Mime brought me up;
Not for the love of me or charity,
But that the child, when come to man's estate,
Should slay for him a dragon in a wood,
Who lay there mounting guard upon a hoard.
He taught me how to forge and how to smelt;
Yet what the craftsman could not do himself
The 'prentice hand achieved, and made a sword
Out of some broken fragments of old steel.
My father's weapon thus I forged anew;

No blade more spick and span than Needful
    now:
Ripe for the battle fancied him the dwarf;
He led me to the wood, and there I slew
The dragon, Fafner.   Mark ye well the tale,
For wondrous things I tell.   Some dragon-blood
Fell on my hand and burned it; in my mouth
I thrust my fingers; hardly had my tongue
Touched the wet blood before I understood
What a bird there sate singing.   Thus he sang:
"To Siegfried now belongs the Nibelung's hoard;
Deep in the cavern he shall find it stored.
If he the Tarnhelm likewise should possess,
'Twill bend to him the nations' haughtiness;
But if he can obtain the magic ring,
'Twill give him power beyond imagining."'
Then Hagen asked: 'So didst thou take away
The ring and Tarnhelm?'   And the vassals said:
'Didst ever hear the little bird again?'
Siegfried made answer: 'I did take away
The Tarnhelm and the ring; I heard again
The pretty warbler, who sang thus to me:
"Tarnhelm and ring are Siegfried's.   Let his heart
Doubt all that Mime saith: the traitor's part
The dragon's blood discloseth."'' 'Was he right?'
Asked Hagen.   And the listening group of men

Shouted : ' How didst thou pay the villain out ? '
Said Siegfried : ' He came nigh with deadly
    drink,
And, pale and stammering, blundered out his
    thought :
Needful fell on him, and the ruffian died.'
Then Hagen laughed : ' The blade he could not
    forge
Poor Mime tasted natheless ! '   And the men :
' What did friend Warbler have to say to that ? '
' First take a draught,' said Hagen, ' from my
    horn ;
For I have mingled juices with the drink
To make thy memory clear, that of the past
Naught may escape thee ! '   So then Siegfried
    drank,
And said : ' I turned me sorrowing to the bough,
Where still he sang : " Dead is the traitor's life,
Fare thou on swiftly to thy destined wife !
Upon the high cold fell Brunhilde sleeps,
Around her fire, undying, vigil keeps ;
If Siegfried through the flaming barrier strove,
Brunhilde would be his in life and love ! " '
' Didst thou obey the counsel of the bird ? '
Asked Hagen.   Siegfried answered : ' Straight
    away

I fared, and tarried not until I found
The fiery fell; I hurried through the flames
And found my prize—a lovely sleeping girl,
In glittering armour clad.   I loosed her helm;
My kisses woke her; O how fervently
Did sweet Brunhilde's arms encircle me!'
'What sayest thou?' cried Gunther furiously,
While from a bush two night-dark ravens flew
Round about Siegfried for a little space,
Then slowly winged their course to father Rhine.
Sneered Hagen: 'Canst thou also read aright
Those ravens' tidings?'   Siegfried started up,
And, looking back towards the distant birds,
He turned his back on Hagen.   This one cried:
'Their   counsel   is   revenge!'   and   plunged   his
        spear
Deep into Siegfried.   Gunther seized his arm;
Too late; the spear had done its bloody work.
Then cried together Gunther and his men:
'Hagen!   what   deed   is   this?'   while   Siegfried
        swung
His shield aloft, as though to crush his foe;
But faintness gat upon his splendid limbs,
And he himself sank down upon the shield.
Then Hagen pointed to the dying man,
And cried: 'I have avenged his perjury!'

Then turned away, and went across the hills.
But Gunther's heart was very sorrowful,
And, bending down by Siegfried, he was 'ware
Of words low spoken in the gates of death.
'Brunhilde! bride from heaven! sleepest thou?
Awake!   Who bound thee down again in sleep?
Who fettered thee in dreamless slumbers drear?
The awakener came, and woke thee with a kiss;
Again he bursts the chains that hold his bride.
Brunhilde's tempting beauty smiles on him!
Ah! those dear eyes, now open for all time!
Ah! the soft pantings of that honeyed breath!
Sweet death! thrice blessèd dread of the un-
    known!
Brunhilde beckons to me: love, I come!'
The faint voice ceased, and Siegfried's spirit fled.

THE HALL OF THE GIBICHUNGS

THE moonlight glinted on the palace walls,
As from her chamber slowly passed Gudrun
And paced the echoing hall.   'Was that his
    horn?
No, no!   Alas! not yet doth he come home.
Bad dreams disturbed my sleep; I heard his
    horse
Neigh wildly; then Brunhilde laughed at me,
And I awoke.   What woman did I see
Hastening towards the river?   How I fear
This fierce Brunhilde!   Is she in her room?'
She listened at a door, and softly called:
'Brunhild'!   Brunhild'!' but no one answered
    her.
Trembling she looked within: 'The room is bare!
Then it was she who went towards the Rhine!'
Startled, she listened to a distant sound.
'Was that his horn?   Nay, all is quiet again:
O that my Siegfried would come back to me!'
Then, on a sudden, Hagen's voice was heard:

'Ho! there within!   Wake up, and fetch me
    lights!
Fetch glowing torches!   Noble game bring we.'
Then Hagen went within the hall, and said:
'Thou here, Gudrun?   Why dost not go to greet
Siegfried?   The hero cometh home to thee.'
Now come, wild-seeming in the flare of brands,
A crowd of men and women, surging round
The bearers of the body of the slain.
And Gunther was among them.   Then Gudrun
Was terrified, and cried: 'Say, Hagen, say!
What's happened?   For I do not hear his horn!'
Her Hagen answered slowly: 'Never more
Will the pale hero sound upon his horn;
Not to the battle, no, nor to the chase
Will he again go proudly; never more
He'll court the favours of the fairest dames!'
Then was the heart of Gudrun turned to stone:
'What do they bring?' cried she.   And Hagen
    said:
'A wild boar's victim; 'tis thy husband's corpse.'
Then Gudrun threw herself upon the bier
With a wild cry, and lay there as one dead.
And Gunther's heart was troubled as he bent
Over his sister, saying, 'Dear Gudrun!
Open thine eyes!   Speak but one word to me!

And when the swoon had passed, Gudrun sate up
And said: 'Siegfried was murdered!   Leave my
    sight,
Thou treacherous brother, slayer of my love!
Horror of horrors! who can comfort me?
My Siegfried have they foully done to death!'
'Reproach not me,' said Gunther, 'Hagen there
Is the accursèd boar who did the deed
And slew this noble heart!'   Then Hagen asked:
'So thou art wroth with me because of this?'
And Gunther answered: 'Grief and misery
Rend thee for ever!'   Then defiantly
Stood Hagen forth, and said: 'Well, then!
    'twas I
Who killed him—Hagen smote him that he
    died!
My spear's spoil was he, on which he swore
False oaths; and thereby have I won the right
Of booty; wherefore do I claim this ring.'
'Stand back,' cried Gunther; 'thou shalt never
    touch
What falleth to my share!'   Then Hagen
    whined:
'My men, ye will not see me hardly used?'
And Gunther mocked him, saying: 'Shameless
    dwarf,

Dost want to steal Gudrun's inheritance ?'
Then Hagen drew his sword, and cried aloud :
' Thus claims the son the dwarf's inheritance !'
And rushed on Gunther.   Savagely they fought,
Not recking of the vassals' outstretched hands,
Till Gunther fell down like a stricken tree,
Stone-dead.   Then Hagen cried triumphantly :
' Now for the ring !' and snatched at Siegfried's
    hand.
But the hand slowly raised itself aloft
With gesture menacing.   Then terror seized
The hearts of all ; the women shrieked aloud ;
And even Hagen paused.   Now suddenly
Brunhilde's voice was heard : ' Let silence fall
Upon your clamorous grief !   The wife betrayed
Is come for vengeance !'   So into the midst
She passed.   ' I heard the children crying out
That milk was spilling from their mothers'
    breasts,
Yet have I heard no word of elegy
Worthy of him who died.'   Then moaned
    Gudrun :
' Brunhilde ! 'tis thy hateful jealousy
Hath brought this thing to pass !   Alas ! the day
When thou cam'st nigh us, for 'twas thou didst
    urge

Those men to do the deed!'   Then said Brun-
    hild' :
' Peace ! thou poor soul !   Thou wast not his
    true wife ;
His paramour wast thou.   I am his wife,
To whom he sware his life's fidelity
Ere ever he saw thee.'   Then cried Gudrun
With the mad passion of a soul's despair :
' Accursèd Hagen !   Ruiner of peace !
Would that to me thou 'dst given the foul drug
That robbed her of her husband !   Grief of
    griefs !
Now know I that Brunhilde was his wife
Whom deadly philtres forced him to forget !'
Shame overmastered her ; she turned away
From Siegfried, and upon the bloody corse
Of Gunther sank down swooning.   Silence fell
Upon them all.   At length Brunhilde spake,
Standing up stately in the very midst—
' Heap up a pyre beside the banks of Rhine ;
Let mighty fires hiss upwards to the sky,
And burn the noble body of the slain.
His horse fetch hither quickly, that with me
His master he may follow, for I long
To share the eternal honour of my lord.
Go ye, and do Brunhilde's last desire !'

Then went the young men to the banks of
    Rhine
And built a pyre, and tearful women strewed
Bright flowers thereon.   And all this time Brun-
    hild'
Kept gazing at the dead face of Siegfried.
' He smiles at me with sunshine in his eyes!
Truest of hearts!   And yet thou couldst be-
    tray!
False to his wife, and faithful to his friend,
He set his sword betwixt him and his bride.
Nobler than he ne'er swore upon his oath;
Truer than he ne'er held to promises;
Purer than he ne'er won a woman's love:
And yet oaths, promises, yea, even love,
Sure none betrayed like him!   And would ye
    know
The secret?   O ye guardians of men's oaths,
Look for a moment on mine agony
And see your deathless shame!   Hear my com-
    plaint
Thou greatest of the gods!   Because he dared
A deed which thine own heart was set upon
Thou gavest him to be the prey of death,
And me the truest living must betray
To make a woman wise!

> Do I know now
What thou wouldst have ? Now is all knowledge
    mine ;
All things are plain ! Thy ravens' wings I hear ;
With tidings long awaited anxiously
I send them home : now rest thee, thou great
    god !'
Then signed Brunhilde to the weeping throng,
And tenderly they lifted up the dead
And set him on the pyre. Then from his hand
Brunhilde drew the ring, and on her own
She placed it, saying : 'Mine inheritance
I take now to myself. Accursèd hoop !
Most terrible of rings ! I hold thee fast,
The better to be rid of thee ! Hear, now,
Ye gliding daughters of the river depths,
The words I speak ! What ye desire I give ;
From out mine ashes take it for your own !
The flames that burn me will destroy the curse
Laid on the ring ; deep in your rushing stream
Melt it, and keep the gleaming lump of gold—
The beaming Star of Rhine—that robbers stole
To our eternal bane.' She turned and took
A flaming firebrand from a vassal's hand.
'Fly home, ye ravens ! Go and tell your lord
What ye have heard beside old father Rhine !

Fly past Brunhilde's fell, where Loge's fires
Still burn, and bid him hurry to the burg!
The dusky twilight closeth round the gods,
And thus I fire Valhalla's citadel!'
She spake, and hurled the torch upon the pyre;
And soon the darting flames roared heavenwards.
'Ye who must live your life's allotted span
Give heed unto my words! When ye have seen
Siegfried and Brunhild' eaten by the flames;
When ye have seen the daughters of the stream
Bear to the depths their well-belovèd ring;
Then look ye through the darkness towards the
    north!
If there the sky is flushed with rosy glow,
Know ye that on Valhalla's end ye gaze!

.   .   .   .   .   .

The race of gods is vanished like a breath,
And masterless I leave the world behind:
The brightest treasure of my wisdom's hoard
I therefore give to you. Not goods, nor gold,
Nor royal pomp, nor palaces, nor halls,
Nor costly shows of wealth's magnificence;
Nor yet the empty kindness of false leagues,
Nor canting custom's merciless decrees:
Care not for these, let Love reign paramount
In sorrow and in joy.'

Then came the men
Leading the horse of Siegfried to Brunhild'.
Swiftly she loosed the bridle from his head,
Then stroked his arching neck, and spoke to
     him :
' How art thou, Grane, who art mine again ?
Dost know where thou art going, dear old
     friend ?
Thy master lies in yonder scorching fire,
Siegfried, my loved one.   Neighest thou to say
That thou art glad to follow ?   Do the flames
Entice thee to his side ?   O feel my breast,
How it doth burn !   My heart is set afire
To throw my arms around him, in his arms
To know the raptures of love's ecstasy !
Greet thou thy master, Grane ; Siegfried dear,
Thy true wife comes to greet thee ! '
                                   Thus she spake,
And leaped upon her horse, who at a bound
Sprang on the burning pyre.   Then hissed the
     flames
Higher and ever higher towards the sky,
And naught to see but molten sheets of fire.
But suddenly the flood-gates of old Rhine
Were loosed, and thundering o'er his ancient
     banks

He swept in giant torrent o'er the pyre.
And now appeared the daughters of the stream,
Gliding where once the fiery terror raged.
Then watching Hagen feared to lose the ring,
And flung away his spear, and eke his helm,
And plunged into the flood. 'The ring is
    mine!'
Cried he; and then the waters covered him.
For twain of those fair sisters of the stream
Twined their soft arms about his neck, and down,
Down went the murderer to the reeds his grave.
Now did Flosshilde hold aloft the ring
With triumph in her eyes, and then below
Sank to the river depths inviolate.
From the far north there streamed a rosy glow;
And so the twilight fell upon the gods.

THE END

Printed by T. and A. Constable, (late) Printers to Her Majesty
at the Edinburgh University Press